Joyce Appleby on *Thomas Jefferson*

Louis Auchincloss on *Theodore Roosevelt*

Jean H. Baker on *James Buchanan*

H. W. Brands on *Woodrow Wilson*

Douglas Brinkley on *Gerald R. Ford*

Josiah Bunting III on *Ulysses S. Grant*

James MacGregor Burns and Susan Dunn on *George Washington*

Charles W. Calhoun on *Benjamin Harrison*

Robert Dallek on *James Monroe*

John W. Dean on *Warren G. Harding*

John Patrick Diggins on *John Adams*

E. L. Doctorow on *Abraham Lincoln*

Annette Gordon-Reed on *Andrew Johnson*

Henry F. Graff on *Grover Cleveland*

Hendrik Hertzberg on *Jimmy Carter*

Roy Jenkins on *Franklin Delano Roosevelt*

Zachary Karabell on *Chester Alan Arthur*

William E. Leuchtenburg on *Herbert Hoover*

Timothy Naftali on *George Bush*

Kevin Phillips on *William McKinley*

Robert V. Remini on *John Quincy Adams*

John Seigenthaler on *James K. Polk*

Hans L. Trefousse on *Rutherford B. Hayes*

Tom Wicker on *Dwight D. Eisenhower*

Ted Widmer on *Martin Van Buren*

Sean Wilentz on *Andrew Jackson*

Garry Wills on *James Madison*

Politics of Continuity

Ambivalent Americans

*Affairs of Party: The Political Culture of Northern
Democrats in the Mid-Nineteenth Century*

The Stevensons: Biography of an American Family

Mary Todd Lincoln: A Biography

Civil War and Reconstruction

Votes for Women

James Buchanan

Jean H. Baker

James
Buchanan

THE AMERICAN PRESIDENTS

ARTHUR M. SCHLESINGER, JR., GENERAL EDITOR

Times Books

HENRY HOLT AND COMPANY, NEW YORK

Times Books
Henry Holt and Company, LLC
Publishers since 1866
115 West 18th Street
New York, New York 10011

Library of Congress Cataloging-in-Publication Data
Baker, Jean H.
    James Buchanan / Jean Baker—1st ed.
        p. cm.— (The American presidents)
    Includes bibliographical references (p.) and index.
    ISBN 0-8050-6946-1
        1. Buchanan, James, 1791–1868. 2. Presidents—United States—
Biography 3. United States—Politics and government—1857–1861. I. Title.
II. American presidents series (Times Books (Firm))
E437.B35 2004
973.6'8'092—dc22
[B]   2003056938

Henry Holt books are available for special promotions and premiums.
For details contact: Director, Special Markets.

First Edition 2004

Printed in the United States of America
1   3   5   7   9   10   8   6   4   2

To Bricks

Contents

Editor's Note

_____

THE AMERICAN PRESIDENCY

The president is the central player in the American political order. That would seem to contradict the intentions of the Founding Fathers. Remembering the horrid example of the British monarchy, they invented a separation of powers in order, as Justice Brandeis later put it, "to preclude the exercise of arbitrary power." Accordingly, they divided the government into three allegedly equal and coordinate branches—the executive, the legislative, and the judiciary.

But a system based on the tripartite separation of powers has an inherent tendency toward inertia and stalemate. One of the three branches must take the initiative if the system is to move. The executive branch alone is structurally capable of taking that initiative. The Founders must have sensed this when they accepted Alexander Hamilton's proposition in the Seventieth Federalist that "energy in the executive is a leading character in the definition of good government." They thus envisaged a strong president—but within an equally strong system of constitutional accountability. (The term _imperial presidency_ arose in the 1970s to describe the situation when the balance between power and accountability is upset in favor of the executive.)

The American system of self-government thus comes to focus in the presidency—"the vital place of action in the system," as Woodrow Wilson put it. Henry Adams, himself the great-grandson and grandson of presidents as well as the most brilliant of American historians, said that the American president "resembles the commander of a ship at sea. He must have a helm to grasp, a course to steer, a port to seek." The men in the White House (thus far only men, alas) in steering their chosen courses have shaped our destiny as a nation.

Biography offers an easy education in American history, rendering the past more human, more vivid, more intimate, more accessible, more connected to ourselves. Biography reminds us that presidents are not supermen. They are human beings too, worrying about decisions, attending to wives and children, juggling balls in the air, and putting on their pants one leg at a time. Indeed, as Emerson contended, "There is properly no history; only biography."

Presidents serve us as inspirations, and they also serve us as warnings. They provide bad examples as well as good. The nation, the Supreme Court has said, has "no right to expect that it will always have wise and humane rulers, sincerely attached to the principles of the Constitution. Wicked men, ambitious of power, with hatred of liberty and contempt of law, may fill the place once occupied by Washington and Lincoln."

The men in the White House express the ideals and the values, the frailties and the flaws, of the voters who send them there. It is altogether natural that we should want to know more about the virtues and the vices of the fellows we have elected to govern us. As we know more about them, we will

know more about ourselves. The French political philosopher
Joseph de Maistre said, "Every nation has the government it
deserves."

At the start of the twenty-first century, forty-two men have
made it to the Oval Office. (George W. Bush is counted our
forty-third president, because Grover Cleveland, who served
nonconsecutive terms, is counted twice.) Of the parade of presidents, a dozen or so lead the polls periodically conducted by
historians and political scientists. What makes a great president?

Great presidents possess, or are possessed by, a vision of an
ideal America. Their passion, as they grasp the helm, is to set the
ship of state on the right course toward the port they seek.
Great presidents also have a deep psychic connection with the
needs, anxieties, dreams of people. "I do not believe," said Wilson, "that any man can lead who does not act . . . under the
impulse of a profound sympathy with those whom he leads—a
sympathy which is insight—an insight which is of the heart
rather than of the intellect."

"All of our great presidents," said Franklin D. Roosevelt,
"were leaders of thought at a time when certain ideas in the life
of the nation had to be clarified." So Washington incarnated the
idea of federal union, Jefferson and Jackson the idea of democracy, Lincoln union and freedom, Cleveland rugged honesty.
Theodore Roosevelt and Wilson, said FDR, were both "moral
leaders, each in his own way and his own time, who used the
presidency as a pulpit."

To succeed, presidents must not only have a port to seek
but they must convince Congress and the electorate that it is a
port worth seeking. Politics in a democracy is ultimately an
educational process, an adventure in persuasion and consent.
Every president stands in Theodore Roosevelt's bully pulpit.

The greatest presidents in the scholars' rankings, Washington, Lincoln, and Franklin Roosevelt, were leaders who confronted and overcame the republic's greatest crises. Crisis widens presidential opportunities for bold and imaginative action. But it does not guarantee presidential greatness. The crisis of secession did not spur Buchanan or the crisis of depression spur Hoover to creative leadership. Their inadequacies in the face of crisis allowed Lincoln and the second Roosevelt to show the difference individuals make to history. Still, even in the absence of first-order crisis, forceful and persuasive presidents—Jackson, Theodore Roosevelt, Ronald Reagan—are able to impose their own priorities on the country.

The diverse drama of the presidency offers a fascinating set of tales. Biographies of American presidents constitute a chronicle of wisdom and folly, nobility and pettiness, courage and cunning, forthrightness and deceit, quarrel and consensus. The turmoil perennially swirling around the White House illuminates the heart of the American democracy.

It is the aim of the American Presidents series to present the grand panorama of our chief executives in volumes compact enough for the busy reader, lucid enough for the student, authoritative enough for the scholar. Each volume offers a distillation of character and career. I hope that these lives will give readers some understanding of the pitfalls and potentialities of the presidency and also of the responsibilities of citizenship. Truman's famous sign—"The buck stops here"—tells only half the story. Citizens cannot escape the ultimate responsibility. It is in the voting booth, not on the presidential desk, that the buck finally stops.

—Arthur M. Schlesinger, Jr.

Introduction

On November 4, 1856, Americans chose James Buchanan, an experienced politician and diplomat, as their fifteenth president. After the election of James Madison in 1808, no president had ever come to office with more impressive credentials. Nor, to this day, has any matched the range of Buchanan's public positions. The Pennsylvanian had served in his state legislature in his twenties, had gone on to the U.S. House and Senate in his middle years, and had interrupted his legislative career to serve in James Polk's cabinet as secretary of state from 1845 to 1849. Earlier Andrew Jackson had appointed him minister to Russia; Franklin Pierce had sent him to the Court of St. James in London as the American minister in the 1850s, and both Polk and his predecessor, John Tyler, had offered Buchanan a seat on the U.S. Supreme Court. As a prominent Democrat proposed for high appointive posts by every Democratic president from the 1820s on, he had been a hopeful contender for a presidential nomination in 1844 and a serious one in 1848 and 1852. Four years later, in 1856, the year in which he was finally nominated, Buchanan led the voting through eighteen roll calls at the Democratic convention.

As a loyal member of the Democratic party, Buchanan represented one of the few remaining national institutions in the United States when he was elected president. By that time, churches had separated into northern and southern factions; newspapers printed only sectional versions of the events of the day, and the new Republican party had no following south of the Mason-Dixon Line. Only the Democracy remained the voice of all the people—North and South. As the male citizens of the American Republic contemplated their presidential choice in 1856, many had good reason to select Buchanan, an "available" man with an outstanding dossier of national and international service, believing he could solve the deepening divide between the sections. "Old Buck" might be just the man to bring harmony to the nation.

Four years later Buchanan left the presidency in disgrace, condemned by Republicans, vilified by northern Democrats, and dismissed even by the southerners whom he had tried so hard to please and whose personal affection he craved. The president, for all his prospects in 1856, had been unable, as he had pledged in his oath of office, to preserve, protect, and defend the Constitution. Despite his promises to resolve the recurring differences over slavery, he had failed. He had divided his party, thereby ensuring the election of the Republican Abraham Lincoln in 1860. And that election led to the secession of South Carolina, followed by six other states in the lower South. A month before Buchanan left office, these seven southern states formed a separate nation, proclaiming themselves the Confederate States of America. On March 4, 1861, when this discredited president traveled home to his estate outside of Lancaster, Pennsylvania, not only had the United States been destroyed; it stood on the brink of a civil war.

Today we see that war as a means to the worthy end of emancipating four million slaves; we view it also as a cathartic final struggle over the meaning of the Union. But such benefits are understood only in retrospect. In 1856 few Americans imagined these contingent, beneficent prospects that might be used to justify Buchanan's presidential performance. Only if one imagines that the success of the Confederate States of America would have long-term benefits for the United States can Buchanan's administration be considered a success.

For Buchanan, it became a point of pride that war did not break out on his watch. While technically correct, in fact he had set the stage for its arrival six weeks after his departure from the presidency. Earlier he had not succeeded in bringing Kansas into the Union as a Democratic state. His Kansas policies had infuriated both northern Democrats and southerners. Nor had he been able to gratify his expansionist obsession of buying Cuba, for it is not only twentieth- and twenty-first-century presidents who view that island with unflagging interest. By every measure except his own—whether that of his contemporaries or later historians—Buchanan was an abysmal failure as chief executive.

The question, then, is why such a well-trained and well-intentioned public figure could have failed so abominably. How could an acknowledged nationalist intent on keeping the Union but who also sympathized with states' rights have done so many things to destroy it? Were the problems over slavery that led to the Civil War insurmountable—beyond the ken of any human to solve—in an age when presidents supposedly viewed themselves as mere administrators executing the laws Congress passed?

Perhaps the disruption of the Union was the result of structural weakness in the U.S. government rather than the fault of any individual. Europeans had always thought the American constitutional arrangement peculiar, with its separation of authority into judiciary, legislature, and executive branches and, so critically for this generation of Americans, state and federal sovereignties. Possibly the four-month period from Lincoln's election in November until his inauguration in March—the so-called lame-duck arrangement established to give representatives time to get to Washington—subverted Buchanan's influence.

Perhaps Buchanan's stubbornly held convictions were the cause of his disasters, especially his inflexible view of the Constitution and his partisan support of the South. Did his legalistic, strict constructionist approach to the executive powers in article 2 of the U.S. Constitution, whereby most domestic authority remained in the hands of Congress and the states, fatally inhibit his resolve in the controversy over the Charleston forts during the winter of 1860? Or did his archaic vision of a slaveholding but undivided nation, increasingly at odds with northern opinion, render him unable to accommodate himself to the direction of the nation? The best American presidents look ahead, even as they shape policies in the present. Buchanan did not. Or perhaps unsatisfactorily for those who wish definitive answers, all these factors were mixed into the unhappy stew of Buchanan's four years in office.

For all of Buchanan's splendid dossier of public service, was this flawed administration the result of the president's deficiencies of character or his age? Today we assess the performance of our chief executives and then deductively posit the ingredients for success. Some historians list ability to communicate with the populace and to direct Congress. Others empha-

size the use of presidential authority to initiate popular pro-
grams that elicit the support of the people. Still others focus
on a president's intellectual strength, integrity, and judgment
at critical moments in our history. Twentieth-century historians make much of a chief executive's emotional intelligence
and political skill, which they combine under the vague head-
ing of leadership. No matter which specific component of
presidential excellence is emphasized, in recent years mental
and psychological stability have emerged as necessary qualifi-
cations for a successful term. What, then, should be said of
Buchanan's character and personality?

This book seeks to suggest some of the reasons for
Buchanan's failure and specifically to explain the gap between
Buchanan's experience and training before his presidency and
his lamentable performance in office, during which, tone-deaf
to the kind of compromises that might have fulfilled his intentions, he blundered on with policies that undermined his
goals. It also imagines Buchanan's failings as possible general-
izations transportable to other presidencies in the nineteenth,
the twentieth, and, indeed, the twenty-first century. Few historians have defended Buchanan's presidency, and the ratings
that habitually place Buchanan among our worst presidents—
along with Pierce, Harding, and Nixon—are not capricious.

Those who defend Buchanan do so by embracing that most
admired of all our presidents, Abraham Lincoln, and arguing
that before the Civil War started, Lincoln followed the same
policies as Buchanan. But although Lincoln inherited Buchanan's choices, he faced different terrain. And for those who
defend Buchanan's peaceful intentions, it is worth remembering that in the crucial episode of his presidency, he agreed to
reinforce Fort Sumter, the federal facility off the coast of

South Carolina, a strategy that in Lincoln's administration led to the outbreak of war.

Stung by the attacks on his presidency, Buchanan spent the last years of his life justifying his administration and drawing out the similarities between his policies and those of Lincoln. He compared his nationalism, especially with regard to keeping the Charleston forts as federal property, to his successor's. He noted how he deplored secession, and he spoke, as did Lincoln, to the perpetuity of the Union. He pointed out that he too had tried to reinforce the flash point of Fort Sumter, although it was a onetime failed mission. But for all his own laborious efforts at a defense of his administration and for those of a handful of mostly fellow Pennsylvanians, James Buchanan remains a fallen idol, impossible to resurrect.

Perhaps this is why so little attention is paid to Buchanan's administration and so much to Abraham Lincoln's. Who wants to read about presidential failures? Who wants to probe one of the greatest of presidential blunders in American history—Buchanan's Kansas policy? Who wants to try to understand Buchanan's retention of disloyal southern cabinet officers who were in touch with the Confederacy, even while they counseled the president on his proper course with regard to the seceded states? Better to focus on history's presidential winners than its losers.

Yet there are important reasons to reexamine Buchanan. First, only in the literal sense did the Civil War begin on April 12, 1861, when the Confederates fired on Fort Sumter. It began in Buchanan's administration. His policies after Lincoln's election in November 1860 were a critical factor in the coming of the war, and he pursued them vigorously. To study Buchanan is to consider why the American Civil War, unthinkable a decade before, became inevitable; why northern Democrats behaved the way they did during the war; and why secessionist southerners, at first a minority in the Confederacy, carried the day. Recent research suggests how contested secession was in the South and indicates how firm policies, such as trying to isolate the secessionists in South Carolina, could have tempered the drive to disunion in other states. But Lincoln has so dominated the story that what happened in Buchanan's administration has obscured the sad, but historically significant, tale of his predecessor.

As Americans try to fathom presidential accomplishment, they need to probe the dismal lessons to be learned from failed administrations. In substantial ways unsuccessful presidencies serve as negative reference points—lessons in avoidance. Critical times often summon forth our best presidents, and it is worth taking the measure of those presidents who, given the opportunity, failed to rise to greatness. James Buchanan was one of these.

1

Ascension—from Stony Batter to the Cabinet, 1791–1848

Born in 1791, James Buchanan was almost as old as the United States, a point of pride throughout his life. The location of his birth, in a log cabin at the foot of North Mountain in the Alleghenies of southern Pennsylvania, was no accident. James Buchanan, Sr., had chosen Stony Batter, in Cove Gap, Franklin County, for its economic opportunities. His decision to live and later buy a trading post there eventually ensured his prosperity.

An orphaned immigrant from County Donegal in northwest Ireland, twenty-two-year-old James Buchanan, Sr., had crossed the Atlantic Ocean in 1783, landing, like many others, in Philadelphia. He had made his way south and west through the rich and expensive farmland to live with an aunt and uncle in York County, Pennsylvania. The Buchanan clan was well known in Scotland and Ireland. Some members had moved from the barren hills of Scotland to Ireland to find a better life than the one they suffered during a period of starvation in the first part of the eighteenth century. Others migrated to protect their freedom of worship as Presbyterians from the assaults of kings and bishops of the Church of England. Ireland proved a way station, and they were soon on the move again, this time across the Atlantic to America.

James Buchanan came with the advantages of education and ambition, though no money. Some of his neighbors later charged that he was a hard bargainer in his financial dealings. Inspired by the implacable doctrine of his Presbyterian faith that he must serve the Lord through hard work and stern duty in this world so that he might find a place in the next, he intended to get ahead. He expected his sons to do likewise. In fact Buchanan exemplified the Scotch-Irish of the so-called fourth migration to America, over a quarter of a million of whom arrived in Pennsylvania and Delaware in the eighteenth century. Some moved across the Susquehanna River into Maryland, Virginia, and Kentucky; others found opportunity in the rich agricultural state of Pennsylvania.

James lived briefly in the town of York with a wealthy uncle who owned a tavern as well as two hundred acres of farmland. There he heard talk of the mountain gap picturesquely named Stony Batter—*batter* is the Gaelic word for road. Five roads intersected there, and the number of horses in transit was sometimes so great as to require a large corral. In this tiny frontier community, there were often so many goods that the place seemed an emporium set in the wilderness. Four years after his arrival, in 1787, the year in which Americans wrote a Constitution and founded a new nation, James Buchanan bought the trading post in Cove Gap where earlier he had served as an apprentice to the owner. Here, for his broker's fee, he sold and bartered finished goods from Baltimore to settlers over the mountains. Then in 1788 he returned to York County to marry Elizabeth Speer, the daughter of a prosperous Scotch-Irish Presbyterian neighbor of his uncle. The next year George Washington took the first presidential oath to preserve, protect, and defend the Constitution. And in what became a civic duty for Americans, citizens of the Republic were encouraged to marry and create families that would lay the foundations of national morality and progress.

James was the second child, and oldest surviving son, of James and Elizabeth Speer Buchanan's large family of eleven children. An older sister died as an infant and, after James, five daughters arrived in the two-year pattern of fecund reproduction accomplished by American wives whose contraception ended when they stopped nursing their infants. Surrounded by younger sisters and an adoring mother who quoted Milton and Shakespeare to her children and engaged them in discussions about public affairs, James occupied a privileged but challenging position in his family. Years later in an unfinished autobiography, he described his father as having great force of character, but he credited his mother for any distinction that he had attained. "She excited [my] ambition, by presenting . . . in glowing colors men who had been useful to their country or their kind, as objects of imitation." Only when he turned thirteen did a younger brother survive. Eventually, three more brothers arrived. One was named George Washington Buchanan. The Republic's first president had become his mother's hero after he stayed in a nearby tavern during the Whiskey Rebellion in 1794–95. Another was named Edward Younger after one of his mother's favorite English poets.[1]

In 1791 James Buchanan, Sr., had moved his family a few miles east—from the rugged isolation of Stony Batter to a large farm near Mercersburg, Pennsylvania. A few years later, in 1794, as his financial circumstances continued to improve, Buchanan uprooted again, this time to a two-story brick home in Mercersburg, a small village populated by eighty families. There he established a store and became a prosperous merchant. At every opportunity he invested in real estate, and soon James Buchanan was the richest man in town.

His wife had urged the move, anxious for the kind of gentility that was impossible on the frontier. Now the Buchanans joined Presbyterian Scotch-Irish neighbors named Campbell, McAllen, and McKinistry. In Mercersburg young James Buchanan attended school in town. At the Old Stone Academy, he studied the traditional classical curriculum of Latin and Greek, along with mathematics and literature and a little history—the standard fare of the private academies of his generation. He was by all accounts, including his own, an excellent student.

With enough money for the leverage of higher education, James Buchanan, Sr., sent his eldest son to Dickinson College in nearby Carlisle, Pennsylvania, where in 1807 he entered the junior class of fourteen students. Throughout his life as a testament to his formality, he had no nickname and was never junior, nor Jim, nor Jimmie except later to his political enemies, who called him "Ten-Cents-a-Day Jimmie" after he supported banking legislation considered unfavorable to workers. At the end of his life and behind his back he became "Old Buck" and "Old Public Functionary," but he remains one of the few American presidents without a nickname. Like his father, he had no distinguishing middle name.

The following year James Buchanan was expelled from Dickinson for bad behavior. Certainly the first half of the nineteenth century was a time of student rebellions in colleges throughout the United States, as riotous youths tested the authority of ministerial presidents and authoritarian institutions. At Yale there was the so-called Bread and Butter Riot; Harvard suffered the Great Rebellion of 1832; and Brown and Princeton endured student rebellions as well. During the disorganized early stages of Dickinson's history, James Buchanan joined a group of noisy classmates who, engaging in collective acts of unruliness, drank at nearby taverns, threw food in the dining room, broke windows, and kept the good citizens of Carlisle awake with their revelry.

It is not the expulsion that is surprising, but rather Buchanan's insistence in his unfinished autobiography that he was not "dissipated" himself, but had drunk, roistered, and disturbed in order to be considered "a clever and spirited youth" by his fellow students. Popularity and the approval of others mattered to this young man, and would throughout his life. Only through the intervention of his Presbyterian rector with the trustees and the Presbyterian minister who was the head of the college was Buchanan reinstated. A year later he graduated with honors, though not the highest honors he thought he deserved. In doing so, he became one of a few thousand young men of his generation to graduate from college. But he never forgave Dickinson, describing the college as "in a wretched condition" when he attended and acknowledging years later that he felt "little attachment to [his] Alma Mater."

For the next stage of his life James Buchanan did not need a college degree, choosing the law as his profession—not, as Woodrow Wilson once said, as the requisite stepping-stone for politics, but in order to earn a living. He moved to Lancaster, a town of eight thousand and at the time the capital of Pennsylvania. As all lawyers knew, the public business of the state and the associations with legislators offered many opportunities to find clients. And there was an even more compelling reason to move to Lancaster. Buchanan had been accepted as a student by the most eminent lawyer in town, James Hopkins. For the next two and a half years he served as an apprentice under the supervision of his well-known and respected mentor. In the custom of the day, Buchanan read and discussed the legal authorities, Joseph Chitty and William Blackstone, as well as the U.S. Codes, the Constitution, and the case law developing around it.

In Buchanan's time there were only three law schools in the United States. Instead the law was a craft, casually handed down from one practitioner to another, who in turn, as Buchanan did after he set up his practice, opened their offices to other young aspirants. It was another seventy years before the American bar and institutions of higher learning created schools for specialized training. Still, Buchanan's self-discipline in learning his chosen profession's habits of orderly thinking and dependence on precedent significantly influenced his political principles and actions. As Buchanan promised throughout his life, he intended to follow the law and the Constitution.

Buchanan gave "severe application" to his studies, becoming a familiar figure in the streets near the courthouse square where Hopkins kept his office. Here the young man walked about, transposing aloud principles of law into his own language and understanding. "I studied the law and only the law," he declared. Later Buchanan acknowledged this process of speaking aloud as the method by which he learned how to give spontaneous political speeches, though in fact most of his speeches were prepared. In 1810, during his first year with Hopkins, his father delivered a stern advisory: "Guard against temptations that may offer themselves," wrote the senior

Buchanan to his son, "knowing that without religion all other things are as trifles and will soon pass away. . . . Go on with your studies and endeavor to be eminent in your profession." And though his father supported all his sons until they became lawyers or clergymen, he informed his eldest son, whom he held to the highest standards of paternal expectation, "[I have suffered] privation in giving you a good education [which] will be compensated by the station in society you will occupy."[2]

Buchanan inherited his lifelong caution from his father. He lacked the sanguine optimism of successful political leaders, who focus on hopeful future solutions for current problems. The aphorisms that shaped his life were grim: "It is the destiny of man to learn that evil treads closely on the footsteps of good"; "Sufficient unto the day is the evil thereof." And while he was considered a good conversationalist, he was never a man of humor.

Soon he established himself as a rising star among Lancaster's twenty-six lawyers, most of whom had to scavenge for clients. By 1812 the city fathers of Harrisburg, in the opinion of those in Lancaster, had stolen the state capital away from a town that was still the largest inland community in the United States. With ambitions as lofty as those of the Buchanan family, Lancaster had expected to be the capital of the United States. Some lawyers quickly uprooted and moved to Harrisburg, Philadelphia, or the growing community of Pittsburgh. But Lancaster remained Buchanan's home for the rest of his life.

After he registered with a notary and passed an informal oral exam given by a committee of the court in that casual arrangement marking the legal accreditation system for this generation, he was accepted into the Pennsylvania bar. A stern teacher, Buchanan now told his own young law apprentices to give up dissipation and bow to his control or face dismissal. His income rose rapidly from less than $1,000 in 1813, the first full year of his practice, to a substantial $11,297 in 1821 (approximately $175,000 today), the year he left Lancaster for Washington as a U.S. congressman. The law was hard work. Buchanan once described the practice that took him to several adjacent counties as "extensive, laborious, and lucrative. It increased rapidly." He was a general-practice lawyer in the Second Judicial District who argued cases in the dusty court-houses of southern Pennsylvania—a jack-of-all-trades who could write wills and contracts, argue guardianship cases for orphans, and litigate property claims. For an ambitious young man, his legal career also had the advantage of putting him in touch with the state's political leaders.

Even as a neophyte, James Buchanan sought high-profile cases that brought prominence, more clients, and larger fees in a circular process that made him, before he was thirty-five, one of the best-known lawyers in southern Pennsylvania. His prudent money management, limited expenses, and adroit land and building investments around Lancaster rapidly made him a prosperous capitalist, worth over $300,000 (nearly $5 million in today's currency) by the time he died, and that after nearly forty-five years in low-paid public service. No doubt with the help of Hopkins, whose statewide reputation guaranteed an overflow of clients, Buchanan emerged as the counsel of choice for several prominent politicians. One colleague described his legal style as straightforward, unimaginative, and tenacious.

When he was twenty-four years old, with only three years' experience, Buchanan defended Judge Walter Franklin in the latter's impeachment trial before the Pennsylvania state senate. A member of the court of common pleas, Judge Franklin had ruled in a classic states'-rights-versus-federal-government controversy that once a militia was nationalized, Pennsylvania's authority over a refusant ended. Accordingly the state could not fine a citizen of Lancaster who had declined to serve in the War of 1812. At a time in American legal history when the distinction between judicial error and impeachable offense rested on party prejudice, judges became hostages for decisions that did not suit the populace. Buchanan, at the time a member of the Federalist party, argued that Judge Franklin had committed no crime or misdemeanor. Franklin might have misjudged the issue, and certainly he had made an unpopular ruling. In his winning argument before the Pennsylvania senate, Buchanan held that only judicial crimes and malfeasance amounted to impeachable offenses.

Outside of court, Buchanan attended to the social necessities required for an ambitious young lawyer on the rise— joining fraternal associations where he met the leaders of the Lancaster community. He became a Mason and later chief master of his lodge; he was a manager for a society ball held in the White Horse Inn, and, most important for his political future, he served as president of the Washington Association, an organization of local Federalists. Like his father, James Buchanan supported that party's program of nationally subsidized internal improvements, protective tariffs, and a U.S. Bank. Soon he was a sought-after speaker who intrepidly—for it was wartime—criticized President James Madison's leadership during the War of 1812. Later, when he was accused of taking positions hostile to those of the Democratic party, Buchanan explained that he had simply followed his father into the Federalists.

Buchanan could make his case against Madison and the War of 1812 with credibility. He had volunteered for a few weeks in a Lancaster company of young men who had no official status as members of the organized militia, but who ended up stealing horses in Baltimore for the American army during the British occupation. In his prolix style, in 1815 James Buchanan charged Madison and his "democratic administration" with "wild and wicked projects": "they had deprived us of the means of defence, by destroying our navy and disbanding our army; after they had taken away from us the power of re-creating them, by refusing the Bank of the United States."

A year earlier Buchanan had won a seat in the Pennsylvania assembly as a Federalist. Twenty-three years old, he was the youngest, though not the quietest, member of the legislature. This success began a string of eleven electoral victories. As he moved up the ladder from state assembly to U.S. Congress and Senate, to the foreign service and the cabinet and finally to the U.S. presidency, he lost only one election, and that as a candidate for the U.S. Senate before the Pennsylvania legislature in 1833. His outstanding record displays his popularity as well as his astute negotiation of the complexities and realignments of his state's party politics. Always he tempered his ambitions with an understanding that the next step in his progression might be the last. Delighted by his first victory—he ran at the top of the ticket—he was cautioned by his father that the interruption of his legal work might destroy his practice. Yet the state legislature met for only three months, and during his first year as a legislator his legal fees doubled. Buchanan knew, even if his father did not, that his contacts at the state level increased his notoriety and brought more clients to his door.

Sometime during this period James Buchanan began a

romance with Ann Coleman, the daughter of the wealthy owner of an iron mine—the richest man in Pennsylvania and a so-called iron master—who lived just down the block from Buchanan's rooms near Court House Square. Coleman shared an important heritage with Buchanan. Like his own father, her father was a rags-to-riches emigrant from County Donegal, with Scotch-Irish Presbyterian roots in the old and new worlds. If Buchanan was a prize local catch with his handsome, whiskerless face (Buchanan never had to shave), blond hair, and six-foot frame, so was Ann Coleman, with her slender body, dark hair, aquiline features, and dark oval eyes. To compensate for a defect in his eyes, Buchanan characteristically leaned his head forward and cocked it to one side. He did this not only because he suffered from wandering eyes—what ophthalmologists today call exodeviation—but because he was also nearsighted in one eye and farsighted in the other. Some observers thought he looked as if he had a stiff neck; others found it an attractive mannerism that made him appear intensely interested in every conversation. At first Ann Coleman was of the latter group and thought he was listening to her, as she was to him. By the summer of 1819 the two were engaged in that informal way in which young Americans of this generation courted and then decided that they would marry. But by the fall the engagement had ended.

Such a disruption in a romance was not unusual at a time when women gave up their freedom and minimal civic standing to become "one" with their husband and, in common law, he the one. Meanwhile men had their own reasons to hesitate before marrying. They worried about their ability to support a wife and their loss of independence, at the same time that they realized the importance of creating a family in the new republic of the United States. The apparent cause of the fracture in Buchanan's relationship was, from Ann Coleman's perspective, negligent treatment by an intended who seemed more interested in his legal and political career than he was in her. Ann informed her suitor that he did not treat her with sufficient attention or affection and that he was only interested in her money. As for Buchanan, his reasons may have involved sexual preference, for there has long been suspicion that our only bachelor president was a homosexual.

Buchanan quickly left town, not in disgrace or embarrassment as a humiliated suitor might, but in order to attend to some business in Dauphin County, where, according to local gossip, he spent time with another woman. Even the rumor of such a dalliance was sufficient cause for Ann to end the engagement. Soon her mother had rushed her off to recover in Philadelphia, where, inexplicably, this previously healthy twenty-three-year-old died suddenly of what one doctor diagnosed as "hysterical convulsions."

When Coleman's father refused to let Buchanan attend the funeral or even walk in the mournful procession that followed his daughter's coffin to the burial ground outside of Lancaster, the former suitor became, as one resident reported, "the whole conversation of the town." Meanwhile Buchanan patronized his future father-in-law with a sympathy note in which the younger man hoped "Heaven would enable you to bear the shock with the fortitude of a Christian." Throughout the winter of 1819, rumors flew about Lancaster, as unfettered as the dry leaves from the town's elm trees. Had Buchanan's fiancée committed suicide after he broke her heart? Was she pregnant? Were the hysterical convulsions epilepsy? Had she taken too much laudanum or chloral hydrate, the latter often used for insomnia? Why had her father refused Buchanan's reasonable request to walk behind the casket? After a few days' seclusion, the subject of the gossip was hard at work on an important case—getting a settlement from the Columbia Bridge Company.[3]

Thereafter Buchanan propagated the myth that he maintained his single status as a measure of devotion to "the only earthly object of my affections." In fact he informed a friend in 1833, when he was in his early forties, that he soon expected to wed. That same year he asked a male friend soon to see "his intended" in person to convey his love. But nothing came of this courtship, suspiciously undertaken during a time when Buchanan was a candidate for the U.S. Senate. In his fifties when he sought a presidential nomination, he considered marriage with a potential first lady, nineteen-year-old Anna Payne, Dolley Madison's niece. But decorum outweighed romance, however patriotic such a union might seem to voters. As he wrote in a rare poetic outburst: "A match of age with youth can only bring/ The farce of winter dancing with the spring." As he aged, Buchanan contemplated his conditions for marriage. What he intended was not a sexual partner but a housekeeper. It was "not good for man to be alone, and [I] should not be astonished to find myself married to some old maid who can nurse me when I am sick, provide good dinners for me when I am well, and not expect from me any very ardent or romantic affection."[4]

In the end James Buchanan never married and so remains the only bachelor among American presidents. Certainly bachelorhood has always been an exceptional and potentially harmful status for any public man in any generation. Before the Civil War only three of every one hundred American men stayed single. Buchanan's celibacy (there was never creditable gossip about his having a sexual relationship with any woman) shaped his personality. His life was never modulated by the need to make compromising adjustments in his domestic affairs, nor did he benefit from the intimacy, affection, and relaxation that a marriage and family might have afforded. An often lonely James Buchanan came to depend on his male friends, and this reliance had a dramatic impact on American history in the winter of 1860. Meanwhile, he absorbed from his unmarried state certain priestly characteristics—a dogmatic narrow assurance of rectitude and celibate virtue, a reserve and distance from even friends and the nieces and nephews who became his wards, and a dependence on the literal word, in his case not of the Bible, but his version of the laws and the U.S. Constitution. When it came time to defend his administration, displaying a remoteness engendered by his lifetime as a bachelor, he wrote about himself in the third person.

In 1821, two years after Ann Coleman died, Buchanan's father was killed in a carriage accident. At the time James had just been elected to Congress, and the sudden death—a victory followed by a loss—seemed to bear out his father's adage that success was often followed by misery. Now there was no one to warn him "of the need to proceed with caution" or to point out "his deficiency in experience." By this time Buchanan did not need reminding of the virtues of hard work. He had also internalized the pessimistic dictum that "the more you know of mankind the more you will distrust them." Returned to Mercersburg to sort out his father's affairs, he found to his irritation that his father had not written a will, and that he was now the head of a family of impoverished, orphaned nieces and nephews.

In 1820, during his first congressional campaign, Buchanan had run as a member of the Republican-Federalist party, the latter a curious mix of labels and beliefs that acknowledged the collapse of the party system into a so-called era of good feelings when there was only one party. During his two terms in the state legislature he had not been much of a Federalist anyway. His opposition to nativist legislation barring naturalized citizens from running for state office led one legislator to encourage him to join Jefferson's and Madison's Republicans. In fact in his early years as a congressman, Buchanan found, as he explained in his unfinished autobiography, no "trace of the old distinction between Federal and Democrat. . . . Several of those elected as federalists held to a considerable extent Democratic principles, while many of those who had been called Democrats held high-toned federal principles."

Meanwhile, during James Monroe's presidency of one-party government, Buchanan's own principles were shifting toward the emerging Democrats. By 1824, in a prescient reading of his congressional district, he was ready to give his allegiance to the political organization that Andrew Jackson was creating. For the rest of his life James Buchanan was an unwavering Democrat, during a period when Americans often changed their party associations. He signed on as a member of the old Jackson school, that group of men in the House of Representatives who, after Jackson lost the presidential election in 1824, gathered loyally around the general and together were the catalyst for the reordering of early-nineteenth-century politics. There Buchanan stayed, as Whigs, Know-Nothings, and, dangerously in his view, Republicans moved onto the political scene. But Buchanan held to the basic Democratic doctrine, in its most simplified and elastic view, of "the Sovereignty of the People, the Rights of the States, and a light and simple Government."

By the 1830s he was "more and more a states rights man." This conviction did not subvert his Unionism. Like many Democrats, Buchanan believed that the United States was the sum of the states. The latter retained authority over most public matters. He repeated the point in 1838: "I am a states rights man, and in favor of a strict construction of the Constitution. The older I grow and the more experience I acquire, the more deeply rooted does this doctrine become in my mind." Buchanan found his philosophical standard in the Tenth Amendment, the last of the Bill of Rights. It held that all powers not specifically delegated to the national government by the Constitution, nor prohibited to the states, remained with the states and the people. Sometimes Buchanan overlooked this last part of the amendment—the power given to the people, not as citizens of the states but as those of the nation.

In Washington for his five congressional terms, James Buchanan joined 211 other congressmen from twenty-four states. What had been a legislative group of sixty-five representatives in the eighteenth century had multiplied, and so had the size of each district. Buchanan's predecessors in the eighteenth century represented thirty-five thousand constituents; Buchanan served over sixty thousand. But the job was easier for him than for most congressmen. Given the proximity of his district to Washington, he had easy access to voters. This ability to travel back and forth became critical to his political success when with Jackson's encouragement he began to organize a Democratic coalition among former Federalist farmers in the northern part of the state, city artisans in Philadelphia, and farmers of Scotch-Irish background, like his own, in the western part of the state. Once the usually dignified, sometimes even haughty James Buchanan stood on a table in the White Swan Tavern in Lancaster, shouting down his noisy opponents as he argued for the Jacksonians and against the despised John Quincy Adams. By 1828, the year of Jackson's election to the presidency, James Buchanan won handily as a Democrat, the party he had worked hard to establish in his home state.

Immediately after his arrival in Washington, Buchanan gravitated toward southerners and away from New Englanders, whom he considered radical extremists. As a bachelor with time on his hands, he found southerners more congenial both socially and ideologically. For a time he boarded with Senator William King of Alabama and ate in a southern "mess" on F Street. In the late 1830s, by then a senator, he lived in Mrs. Ironsides's boardinghouse on Tenth near F Street, again with King. So intimate was he with the handsome Alabama senator, who was known as a dandy in his home state and an "Aunt Fancy" in Washington, that one congressman referred to the two men as "Buchanan & his wife" in a reference to their bachelor status, which also hinted at their homosexuality.

On the basis of slender evidence, mostly the circumstances of his bachelorhood and three asides by contemporaries about his effeminacy, Buchanan has been dubbed America's first homosexual president. Referring to his femininity, Andrew Jackson once called him an "Aunt Nancy." In an age when women could not vote, such a charge held political as well as sexual implications. There is also evidence that Buchanan's niece Harriet Lane and King's niece Catherine Ellis destroyed their uncles' letters to each other when Buchanan became president. While the existing correspondence between King and Buchanan conveys the affection of a special friendship—in one Buchanan wrote of his "communion" with his roommate—so do the letters of many notably heterosexual nineteenth-century men. Absent the discovery of new material, no one will ever know whether Buchanan and King (the only man to whom his name was ever erotically connected) had sexual relations.

In any case this was a period before the word *homosexual* had come into use, and before Americans identified themselves as straight, gay, or, in some instances, both. Men in Buchanan's time did not have sexual identities, although they did have sexual behaviors. Certainly both King and Buchanan knew that men occasionally had sex with each other. They read about it in the Bible, in New York's sporting newspapers, and in the sex manuals of the period, even if as lawyers they did not follow the court cases that involved punishment for homosexual activity.[5] They also knew that such relationships were against the law, and Buchanan may have been too ambitious to jeopardize his career in this way. The best speculation about the sexuality of the nonshaving Buchanan, who in his portraits has eunuchlike, endomorphic features of body and face as well as the low hairline characteristic of asexual men with low levels of testosterone, is that he had little interest in sex. What is important in his story is the deep friendship that he maintained with the southerner King from the time of their first acquaintance until the latter's death in 1853.

Besides King, the legislators James Buchanan most admired were southerners like William Lowndes of South Carolina, Philip Barbour of Virginia, and even the eccentric John Randolph of Virginia. During the 1830s when he was a senator, he continued to board with King and two Virginians, not—as was typical of other congressmen and senators, including the Pennsylvania delegation—with fellow residents of his state or another nearby state with similar interests.[6]

From the beginning of his congressional service Buchanan complained that the reputation of some attention-getting members exceeded their actual contributions. Others, he grumbled until he started doing the same thing, gave speeches intended for home consumption rather than for the enlightenment of the House. Six weeks after he was sworn in, Buchanan risked a first speech on a safe subject, in this case on the patriotic necessity of passing a military appropriations bill to pay the army.

The effort was a harbinger of his future speeches. Never witty or ironic and seldom facile in debate, he depended on careful preparation, evidence, rebuttal, and occasional flights of sentimental rhetoric. His was the oratory of a lawyer. At the end of a nearly four-hour speech on the Bankruptcy Bill in which he argued against extending its protections to farmers, he included some traditional populist boilerplate: "Experience has taught us a lesson which, I trust, we shall never forget—that a wild and extravagant spirit of speculation is one of the greatest curses that can pervade our country. Do you wish again to witness the desolation which has spread over the land? . . . the road to wealth and honor is not closed against the humblest citizen and Heaven forbid that it ever should be! It is however the destiny of man to learn that evil often treads closely upon the footsteps of good." Proudly, he reported that he was heard by the whole chamber, an important consideration at a time when even if the members were disposed to listen, they could not hear, given the acoustics in "Old Statuary Hall." To be heard "requires great compass of voice and stentorian lungs."

In his ten years as a congressman Buchanan gained the reputation of a middling man in terms of ability and influence. He
was not in that first-rank group of most influential members
like Henry Clay, John C. Calhoun, and Daniel Webster whose
inspirational speeches filled the galleries. In fact Clay enjoyed
baiting the Pennsylvanian, considering him inept and unimaginative and on one occasion mercilessly referring to his crossed
eyes. "I often suppose that the gentleman [Buchanan] is looking at me when in fact he looks quite the other way," after
which Clay crossed his fingers. In another debate Clay noted
that Buchanan had lived thirty-five years without taking "any
fair lady" under his protection. But Buchanan was not one of
the invisible, the speechless, the incompetent, or the alcoholic
representatives who came to Washington during this period.
Appointed to the Committee of Agriculture his first year, he
later rose to be chairman of the House Judiciary Committee.[7]

As had been the case in Buchanan's early years as a lawyer,
an impeachment case brought him to the attention of Congress. Judge James Peck of Missouri had high-handedly dis-
barred and sent to prison a St. Louis attorney who had
publicly criticized several of his decisions. The House had
refused to prosecute Peck until Buchanan became chairman of
the Judiciary Committee and the chief manager of the prosecution. By this time Buchanan had narrowed his understanding of the boundaries between judicial error and malfeasance,
arguing the prosecution's case against Peck. Contending that
Peck had intentionally violated the U.S. Constitution and the
laws of the land, he argued that the judge had abused his judicial authority. There was "criminal intention on his part." An
acquittal would be, said Buchanan to the Senate in May 1830,
"a hopeless, remediless submission to judicial usurpation and

tyranny." But enough of the Senate thought otherwise and acquitted Peck by one vote.

Buchanan's greatest service during his decade in Congress reflected both his legal mentality and his former Federalist principles. In his last session as a congressman, he refused to accept the majority position of the Judiciary Committee of which he was chairman. Without his agreement, its members had drawn up a bill to repeal the twenty-fifth section of the 1789 Judiciary Act. The latter gave the Supreme Court appellate and original jurisdiction over state cases when the Constitution, treaties, and laws of the United States were in question. Limiting the federal judicial power to the cases that arose in federal court under original jurisdiction would have severely truncated the court's national authority. As Buchanan informed the House, there would be no uniformity to the interpretations of the Constitution, and "an authority higher than that of the sovereign states would be overlooked." That power was, as it always would be for Buchanan, the sovereign authority of the people as expressed through their state ratifications of the Constitution, the latter document then becoming the supreme law of the land. When the House defeated the bill to repeal, Buchanan, an avowed believer in states' rights, nevertheless acknowledged a victory for national unity and federal sovereignty.

Buchanan entered Congress after the passage of the Missouri Compromise, the first of several legislative negotiations over slavery. The compromise balanced the number of slave and free states at twelve and temporarily settled the issue of slavery in the territories by drawing a line across the United States at the 36° 30′ latitude. Above this point there could be no slavery. Three decades later Buchanan still hoped that this arrangement would forever end disagreements over slavery, but he was far too optimistic. For the rest of his life, in one form or another, slavery defined public discussion in America. One need look no further than Buchanan's public career for evidence that slavery was the central cause of the Civil War. It was the albatross neither he nor the nation could ever shake.

Even during a congressional debate in 1830 over a proposed mission to Panama, an issue seemingly far removed from the South's peculiar institution, slavery intruded. In his long speech on the advisability of the mission, Buchanan digressed, holding slavery to be a political and moral evil, but an evil without a remedy. Emancipate the slaves in the United States and "they would become masters. . . . Is there any man in this Union who could for a moment indulge the horrible idea of abolishing slavery by the massacre of the high-minded and the chivalrous race of men in the South?" Buchanan had already chosen sides. He would never desert the "chivalrous race" of white men in the South. Thirty years before the coming of the Civil War he had "buckled on [his] knapsack and marched in defence of [the white southern] cause" by opposing any interference with slavery.

In 1831 James Buchanan declined a sixth nomination to Congress from the loyal Democrats in his Pennsylvania district of Dauphin, Lancaster, and Lebanon counties. He preferred, he informed his brother George Washington Buchanan, to return to private life. Yet he remained politically ambitious and hoped to be on the rise again after his ten years in Congress. At the time some Pennsylvanians were bruiting his name about as a possible vice presidential nominee to run with Andrew Jackson in the presidential election of 1832. But Jackson chose Martin Van Buren and offered Buchanan the lesser plum of the Russian ministry.

Buchanan hesitated, giving as his reason the transparent excuse that he could serve Jackson more "usefully" from his vantage point as a prominent leader in Pennsylvania. In fact the mission seemed an exile from the public affairs that were the center of his life, and was intended as such by the president, who once called Buchanan "an inept busybody." Moreover, Buchanan did not speak French, the language of diplomacy. Nor could he leave his private business. He might have added that his mother was opposed. She had begged him to refuse this appointment, noting his previous successes—his "gratifying" political career and "the pecuniary matters [that] are no object to you."[8] But when James Buchanan learned that he would not have to leave until the breaking of the ice in St. Petersburg the following spring, he accepted.

For eighteen months Buchanan ran the American ministry in St. Petersburg, diligently working on his assignment to negotiate both a commercial and a maritime treaty with the Russians. He succeeded in the first and gained President Jackson's gratitude. But any maritime treaty involving the principle "free ships make free goods" proved elusive, as Buchanan tirelessly trekked from the ministry to the offices of his counterpart, Count Nesselrode. During his months in Russia he learned French and enjoyed his magnificent view of the Neva along with high society, which included an audience with Czar Nicholas I. He also absorbed the lesson that diplomacy and statesmanship proceeded slowly. As a good democrat from America, he disliked the closed nature of Russian society, its censorship, the Russians' profanity even on Sundays, the government's spies, and the terrible treatment of the serfs. He was thankful, after eighteen months, to return home to Lancaster. But while he was abroad both his mother and one of his brothers had died.

Pennsylvania Democrats also missed James Buchanan. Although he lost the election in the state legislature for a full senatorial term of six years in the winter of 1833, the state legislature picked him to fill the shorter term of a Democrat who had replaced him in St. Petersburg. So began Buchanan's service as a U.S. senator, which lasted from December 1834 to March 1845. When he was reelected in 1836 and 1842, his growing national reputation and the fact that no Pennsylvanian had ever been president stoked Buchanan's supreme aspiration—to be president of the United States. For this he needed a united Democratic party in Pennsylvania, and demanded that the state's party convention unanimously pass a resolution supporting him as their favorite son. But it was unseemly to acknowledge such ambition. So Buchanan told his friends that the U.S. Senate was the only "distinction" to which he aspired.

Yet he gave interviews to newspaper editors and wrote endless letters to state and national leaders from a list he kept in little black notebooks. Buchanan correctly anticipated that his dutiful service as a Democrat in the Senate would enhance his national reputation. As a loyal Jacksonian, he opposed the rechartering of the U.S. Bank ("a despotic monied corporation. . . . The Democratic party must either triumph over the Bank or the Bank will crush the Democracy"). He supported Van Buren's Subtreasury plan to move public funds from the U.S. Bank into a separate government depository. He argued against Senator John C. Calhoun's proposal for a gag rule preventing Congress from receiving abolitionist petitions. "We have just as little right to interfere with slavery in the South, as we have to touch the right of petition. . . . Can a republican government exist without it? The people have the right to make their wants and rights known to their servants," he said in a three-and-a-half-hour speech in January 1836 that must have tried the patience of even his mutually long-winded fellow senators, given its repetitiveness and digressions. Although Jackson, who believed Buchanan lacked courage, never forgave the Pennsylvanian for what the president incorrectly interpreted as Buchanan's support of Clay in the ferociously contested 1824 election, Buchanan was ever the dutiful senator. He even sought to expunge the ill-tempered congressional resolution that had censured Jackson for his removal of deposits from the U.S. Bank.

By the 1840s Buchanan had taken an inflexible position on slavery. Quietly opposed to the institution in theory for reasons he never explained, he believed it the nation's weak link, not because it was inhumane, but rather for its potential to destroy the Union. "Touch this question of slavery and the Union is from that point dissolved." For the bachelor Buchanan, slavery emerged as a domestic affair in two senses—first, because it was under the constitutional jurisdiction of the states as a local matter, and second, because it affected the families of southerners. Adopting the southern view that black male slaves were potential rapists, he held the "excitement over slavery" to be the fault of abolitionists. Their movement, he concluded in one of his strikingly inaccurate predictions, was "weak, powerless, and soon to be forgotten."

Forty-three years old when he first took his seat as a U.S. senator, Buchanan moved to the front ranks of senatorial prestige. He debated the great men of this era: John C. Calhoun of South Carolina, Daniel Webster of Massachusetts, Henry Clay of Kentucky, and Thomas Hart Benton of Missouri. He was a politician who avoided the kind of maneuvering that left many men languishing in political backwaters. Astutely, he turned down President Martin Van Buren's offer of the attorney generalship in 1838. Throughout his years in the Senate he held fast to two popular principles: manifest destiny and states' rights. Of the latter, he informed his fellow senators in April 1836: "The older I grow, the more I am inclined to be what is called a 'State Rights man.' The peace and security of this Union depend upon giving to the Constitution a literal and fair construction, such as would be placed upon it by a plain, intelligent man, and not by ingenious construction, to increase the powers of this government, and thereby diminish those of the States. The rights of the States reserved to them by that instrument ought to be held sacred."

Through hard work, party loyalty, and residence in the second most populous state in the Union, Buchanan advanced in stature and position, moving up the committee ladder to ever more important positions and ever more national notoriety. He was appointed to the Judiciary Committee, the Committee on the District of Columbia, and eventually the Senate Foreign Relations Committee. It was as a member of the latter that he became best known and made his most significant contributions to the future of the nation.

From its beginnings the United States had embraced as one of its values national expansion. All presidents believed that the movement of Americans westward was inevitable, divinely ordained, and economically beneficial. Jefferson had purchased the huge Louisiana Territory from the French; Madison had sent the marines into Spanish-controlled Florida and had invaded Canada during the War of 1812; and Jackson owed his political popularity to his military service against the Creek Indians and the British. From 1790 to 1860 no decade passed without an increase in the number of states incorporated into the Union. All Democrats of this period and most Whigs were territorial expansionists, but none was so fervent as James Buchanan, whose speeches have come to summarize what we now call "manifest destiny."

Indeed Buchanan's statements are textbook examples of the justifications for the spread of the United States across the continent and, beginning in the 1840s, into Mexico and Central America. "This I believe," he said in 1837. "Providence has given to the American people a great and glorious mission to perform, even that of extending the blessings of Christianity and of civil and religious liberty over the whole North American continent. Within less than fifty years there will exist one hundred millions of free Americans between the Atlantic and Pacific Oceans. . . . What, sir! Prevent the American people from crossing the Rocky Mountains? You might as well command Niagara not to flow. We must fulfill our destiny."

Buchanan translated his rhetoric into action. In 1841 he became one of only nine senators to vote against the Webster-Ashburton Treaty, a widely applauded Anglo-American pact fixing the northern border between Maine and Canada. Buchanan wanted more land and attacked what he called Secretary of State Daniel Webster's cowardly surrender of eight thousand square miles. Buchanan claimed for the United States the entire Aroostook Valley in what today is the Canadian province of New Brunswick. The "dishonorable" treaty, he informed the Senate in June 1841, was unfair to Maine and an "unqualified surrender . . . to British dictation."

The expansionist instincts of many senators were restrained by their sectional bias. Those from the nonslaveholding northern states supported expansion into Canada and Oregon, and those from slaveholding southern states favored the addition of Texas and parts of Mexico and Central America, but not the reverse. Buchanan fought for territory everywhere. He claimed the American right to possess territory in Oregon up to the 54° 40' latitude. And in his last long speech to the Senate in February 1845, he made the case for the annexation of Texas on three grounds. First, Texas, now independent of Mexico, deserved to be a part of "our glorious Confederacy." (The term *confederacy* was commonly used at the time for the entire Union.) Second, the state would be a perfect dumping ground for slaves. Fearful of slave uprisings, he was convinced that slaves from the cotton South would be absorbed into Texas in areas growing corn and wheat and raising cattle, while economically useless slaves would drift into Mexico, where they would be assimilated into that nation's already "darker-hued" population. Finally, Buchanan believed that a sovereign, independent Texas would invite troublemaking British intervention. But once in the Union, the state could be divided into five slaveholding states, thereby balancing any new free states in the North. "Shall Texas become part of our glorious confederacy or shall she become our dangerous and hostile rival? Shall we drive her away in despair to form alliances with strangers?"

Some of Buchanan's contemporaries complained that his extraordinary ambitions for territorial enlargement marched in step with his assessment of public opinion and his eagerness for the presidency. Certainly no Democrat exceeded his commitment to expansion, a popular position by the 1840s, but one that fewer and fewer politicians from the northeastern and Middle Atlantic states accepted. Stalwarts of manifest destiny came from the West and the South. As a Pennsylvanian, Buchanan was out of step with his section, in part because he desperately wanted the presidency and recognized the popularity of expansionism with his principal clients—the southerners. Additionally, his ministry in Russia, where his intended plan for a maritime rights treaty had been flummoxed by Great Britain, taught him the opportunistic nature of British colonialism and made him sensitive to the potential danger of English meddling in Oregon, Texas, and Mexico.

Throughout the 1840s and 1850s Buchanan proclaimed himself a states' rights man, but it was as a nationalist that he fought and voted for, and as a diplomat shaped the boundaries of, the continental United States. In the case of the taking of land claimed by other nations and not sanctified by the loss of American blood, Buchanan held the popular view that the United States was exceptional. Its commitment to freedom justified the liberation of Oregon, California, Mexico, parts of Central America, and Cuba from inferior regimes and European governments that in the future might threaten the United States. In the jingoistic language of his generation's Democrats, Buchanan marshaled all the contemporary arguments for manifest destiny from natural right, geographic proximity, and destined use of the soil to the extension of freedom, the blessings of Christian civilization, God's will, and self-defense.

In 1844 Buchanan hoped that he might win the Democratic nomination for the presidency, and this year, unlike 1836 and 1840, he began a letter-writing campaign to the leaders of state parties, offering himself as a candidate if Martin Van Buren withdrew. Although deferential submission to the people's will was giving way to more aggressive personal campaigning, Buchanan was reluctant to curry voters' support. Instead he sought to be chosen by the sovereign people without seeking the nomination. Of course this was something of both a fantasy and a fiction, given the activity of his friends to ensure that Pennsylvania's Democratic Convention unanimously resolved that he was their choice. As a senator he held himself to be a representative of the people—a trustee, as it were—available to be instructed by them through the state legislature as to his votes in Congress. With duty foremost, several times in his ten years as a senator Buchanan dutifully followed the instructions of the state legislature and voted, with some embarrassment, against positions he espoused in his speeches.

To Buchanan's chagrin, a disciple of Andrew Jackson from Tennessee, James K. Polk, won the nomination and the election in 1844. Promptly, for this was a generation that believed in defusing the threat of competitors by placing them in the cabinet, Polk nominated Buchanan as his secretary of state. The president was also rewarding the Pennsylvania senator for his hard work during the campaign. Traditionally the position was the premier seat in the cabinet, especially since the Democrats had pledged themselves, with careful attention to their language, to the reoccupation of Oregon and the reannexation of Texas. These were goals that Buchanan enthusiastically embraced.

Buchanan accepted Polk's offer, though after a few months he decided he would prefer to sit on the Supreme Court. Three vacancies on that bench had occurred in the two years from 1843 to 1845; two justices had died, and the famed Justice Joseph Story, in his mid-sixties and in poor health, had resigned. Polk's predecessor, John Tyler, had already offered Buchanan one of these seats. He had declined, but then a few months after his confirmation by the Senate as secretary of state, Buchanan changed his mind and asked Polk to appoint him to the Court. At James Buchanan's annual grand ball in January 1846, the chatter among the thousand guests gathered at Carusi's saloon was that their host would leave Polk's cabinet for the bench. A month later, fearful that he might not be confirmed, Buchanan withdrew the request he had made two months before.

Then in June 1846 he again asked for a Supreme Court appointment, informing his brother Edward: "It is now more than possible that I shall go upon the Bench near the close of the present session of Congress. All things considered, I believe this to be the best." A few weeks later he reversed himself, convinced that such a position would hurt his presidential chances, but publicly acknowledging the importance of his serving the administration by staying in the cabinet. "I cannot desert the President." Despite his frequent disavowals of interest in the presidency, Buchanan knew that no one had ever moved from the Court to be chief executive, and he was not a man to test precedent.

Polk was glad enough to have Buchanan stay in the cabinet, because his hardworking secretary of state, as Polk wrote in his diary, "had shown a willingness to carry out my views instead of his own." Still, the president found Buchanan "brooding, in a bad mood, not pleasant in his intercourse with me." Polk attributed this crankiness to Buchanan's indecision about what to do. Buchanan, wrote Polk in his diary in August 1846, "would rather be Chief Justice of that Court than be President of the United States. He said that he did not desire to be a President and never had." At the time this disavowal astonished Polk, the Democrats of Pennsylvania, and most of Buchanan's friends in the Senate. "For God's sake stay where you are," wrote one political friend anxious for a patronage appointment. By December 1847 Buchanan's presidential ambitions had revived. As part of his campaign for the Democratic nomination in 1848, he initiated a series of dinners, given every ten days at Carusi's during the Washington social season, to which, at his own expense, he invited party leaders, lobbyists, and influential patronage holders.[9]

In the end Buchanan remained secretary of state for the duration of Polk's administration. From 1845 to 1849 this zealous exponent of manifest destiny presided over the largest increase in territory in the history of the United States. When Polk came to the presidency, the United States consisted of twenty-six states and 1,787,880 square miles; when he left, an additional 1,204,740 square miles had been added, from which the remaining twenty-two continental states would be created. Buchanan had wanted even more. Most of this was the result of the absorption of territory from Mexico and from Oregon, jointly occupied in 1818 by the Americans and the British, both of whom awaited a negotiating advantage.

Polk and Buchanan agreed about the overall strategy of this expansion, but they often disagreed over tactics and particulars. Sometimes they ended up exchanging positions. Buchanan, who was four years older than the less-experienced president, never hesitated to oppose Polk, whom he considered ill-trained and sometimes poorly informed about the precise matters of geography that Buchanan knew so well. At first Buchanan argued for settling with the British in Oregon at the forty-ninth parallel, while Polk insisted on more territory. Meanwhile northern Democrats were beginning to rally around the slogan "54° 40' or fight," the latter a claim to a latitude north of Fort Simpson in the British territory of Canada.

Rapidly converted, Buchanan now took the position that American honor was involved in a diplomatic contest over territory that, in reality, only trappers and hunters had explored and that some thought unfit for settlement. But, according to Buchanan, "War before dishonor is a maxim deeply engraved upon the hearts of the American people." Pulling the lion's tail, the American secretary insisted that the United States held a legitimate claim to most of Oregon. If Britain did not give way, he said, war was justified and "may we anticipate the smiles of heaven upon the right," he wrote a friend in July 1845. Meanwhile Polk had converted as well, but in the opposite direction. Eventually Buchanan deferred to the president's position, and the boundary between Canada and the United States was set at the forty-ninth parallel.

An overburdened Buchanan, who compared himself to a galley slave, had to deal simultaneously with Mexico, where warfare erupted over a boundary dispute in 1846. As a member of the Polk administration, he supported the dubious proposition that Mexicans had attacked American troops on U.S. territory across the Rio Grande. Earlier Polk, Buchanan, and other Democrats had laid the groundwork for American aggression by pointing to Mexico's instability and the resulting opportunity for British meddling.

During the brief conflict Buchanan cautiously advised Polk against taking any Mexican territory below the Rio Grande or south of New Mexico, on the grounds that "the opinion of the world would be against us." On the other hand, Polk and the rest of his cabinet wanted to extend the national boundary deep into Mexico, down to the twenty-second parallel. By 1848, after the Americans had occupied Mexico in the course of the eight months of actual fighting, Buchanan shifted his position, opposing a peace treaty with the Mexicans that he believed provided an insufficient indemnity. After all, the war, in his and Polk's judgment, had been Mexico's fault. Now Buchanan stubbornly argued against Polk and the rest of the cabinet that the United States should take several provinces along the line of the Sierra Madre as well as all of lower California. He had always supported the annexation of California, but now he wanted to add at least twenty thousand square miles to the southern border of New Mexico. He also insisted that the mouth of the Colorado River in the Gulf of California be included in any settlement.

"Mr. Buchanan's opinions have evidently undergone a change in the course of a few weeks or rather he seems to be now in an unsettled state of mind," wrote Polk in his diary. And the president thought he knew why, given the popularity of claims for more territory. "Since he has considered himself a candidate for the Presidency it is probable he looks at the subject with different considerations in view from those which he entertained before that time. . . . I deemed it my duty to remind Mr. Buchanan of his total change of opinion and position," to which Buchanan replied that the costs of the Mexican-American War in blood and money justified his desire for more land. Yet Buchanan's was a minority voice—no one else in the cabinet was running for president—and the Treaty of Guadalupe Hidalgo, surrendering five hundred thousand square miles of former Mexican territory, was accepted by the Senate and signed by the president in February 1848.

Clearly, Buchanan had taught Polk a lesson in this election year in which Zachary Taylor, the Mexican-American War's conquering hero, became the Whig party candidate: "No candidate for the presidency ought ever to remain in the cabinet.

He is an unsafe advisor," concluded the president, who was more convinced than ever that Buchanan did not want to offend southerners intent on claiming more slave states. In the final analysis, wrote Polk of the man who had served for four years as his secretary of state, "Buchanan is an able man, but is in small matters without judgment and sometimes acts like an old maid."[10]

Buchanan spent part of 1848 working for the Democratic nomination. A newspaperman described his quiet campaign as a "still hunt for the Presidency . . . never did a wily politician more industriously plot and plan to secure a nomination than Mr. Buchanan did."[11] But at the Democratic National Convention in May, a disappointed Buchanan commanded only the Pennsylvania and Virginia delegations and a few scattered votes. On the fourth ballot Senator Lewis Cass of Michigan won the Democratic nomination.

Certainly Buchanan, as he returned temporarily to private life, had made his mark on American history, but neither his hopes for higher office nor his expectations for enlarging the United States were satisfied. As he wrote the incoming secretary of state, John Clayton: "We must have Cuba. We can't do without Cuba, and above all we must not suffer its transfer to Great Britain. We shall acquire it by a coup at some propitious moment. . . . Cuba is already ours. I feel it in my finger tips." It was four years before James Buchanan came back to Washington, and when he did, he had not forgotten Cuba or the presidency.

2

Wheatland to the White House,
1849–1856

In the spring of 1849 James Buchanan went home to Lancaster. For the first time in over thirty years he held no public position nor any prospects save those that represented demotions or repetitions for a man who had served in the highest echelons of his nation's offices. Buchanan declined a half-hearted solicitation by a group of Pennsylvania Democrats to run for the U.S. Senate. And he had no chance for a patronage appointment. Despite his efforts, the 1848 presidential election had swept the Whig ticket of Zachary Taylor and Millard Fillmore into office with 47 percent of the popular vote in a three-way race. With the triumphs of the recent Mexican-American War fresh in their minds, even some of Pennsylvania's faithful Democrats had shifted their support to the war hero Taylor, whose political views were vague, although his victories at the battles of Palo Alto and Buena Vista remained vivid national memories. And while Buchanan believed the third party—the Free-Soilers, who were committed to no more slave states or slave territory—a temporary and dangerous aberration, 10 percent of the American electorate supported its candidate, former president Van Buren.

Leaving Washington in March 1849, Buchanan informed friends who had hoped to organize a dinner in his honor: "You have not overrated the fidelity with which I have discharged my duties to the Country, in Congress and the State Department." His motivation for this excellent performance had been his devotion to Democratic principles, which he had "promoted and defended." In what became a theme in the coming years, Buchanan held his party to be the sole protector of an increasingly sectionalized Union. Devoted to solutions of the past, he never appreciated the determination not only of abolitionists, who wanted to end slavery, but of those northerners who saw the South as an aggressor. As leader of a party whose strength lay with slaveholders, he discounted the moral and political anachronism that slavery was becoming.

In Buchanan's view, Democrats had brought "liberty, order, and unexampled prosperity at home." Any change in party would "excite dangerous jealousies and divisions among the states." The latter was classic Buchanan boilerplate for any shift in policies regarding the return of fugitive slaves and the protection of slavery before statehood in the new territories. Ironically, these new claimants for statehood where slavery was such a flammable issue were Buchanan's personal legacy to the nation's expansion.

Fifty-eight years old in 1849, Buchanan had spent the best years of his life in public office. During that time he had changed from an energetic party enthusiast into an overweight, ambivalently ambitious politician. The newspapers had taken to calling him "Old Public Functionary," and though he was not a joking man, sometimes he referred to himself by the initials O.P.F. With his tilted head, protruding stomach, proportionally diminutive lower body, and heavily lidded eyes, one sometimes shut, he resembled an erect, two-footed tyrannosaur. Antislavery northerners believed his principles to be Neanderthal. Unlike most American men of his age and station, who favored black bow ties, Buchanan customarily wore a high white collar with a white handkerchief that over-flowed onto the lapels of his morning coat. His clothes, identical to those of public men two generations earlier, were another reflection of his old-fashioned tastes.

For the next four years Buchanan turned his attention to his personal life, buying a home on the outskirts of Lancaster. He paid $6,750 for Wheatland, named by its previous owner for its setting on a hill amid the lush grain fields of southern Pennsylvania. Henceforth it served as his northern version of the plantations of his southern friends. In fact when it came time for his 1856 campaign biography intended for extensive circulation in the South, a handsome lithograph of the estate figured prominently in the Buchanan story. A massive three-story brick house with twenty-two rooms and several outbuildings including a carriage house and extensive garden set on twenty-two acres, Wheatland was far too large for a bachelor.

But by this time several of Buchanan's brothers and sisters and their spouses had died or were penniless, and he had become the center of a kinship network of twenty-two nieces and nephews as well as, by 1852, thirteen grandnieces and grandnephews. Seven of these were orphans under his legal guardianship, while others had one surviving parent and depended on him for financial support. He ran a family employment agency, dunning his political friends for patronage positions for some of his nephews as government clerks and, once, for a position in the Revenue Cutter Service. Many of these cousins spent summers at Wheatland, where he counseled them in the gruff paternalistic style that masked his genuine affection. For his most preferred nieces and nephews he became a conscientious surrogate parent, offering advice and finding them foster parents among his Lancaster friends when he was in Washington. The orphaned Harriet Lane, his favorite sister's youngest daughter, emerged as the most favored among the sons and daughters of Buchanan's sisters and brothers. When Buchanan moved to the White House in March 1857, Harriet Lane became his first lady, so designated in the first use of that term because she was not his wife, but rather his official lady and hostess.

She called him "Nunc," and throughout her adolescence and early adulthood, Harriet Lane received, in exchange for his special favor and her residence in Wheatland, incessant prescriptions for proper behavior. "Your day will come," he once wrote an impatient Harriet, who wanted to go visiting. "After your education shall have been completed and your conduct approved by me," he promised to introduce her to the world "in the best manner." He intended her to be amiable, intelligent, and sensible, like the younger, usually southern women he enjoyed flirting with on his social rounds in Washington and Lancaster. Sometimes he took Harriet with him to Bedford Springs in western Pennsylvania for his annual two-week holiday in August; there, as he aged, he found "fewer and fewer of the old set . . . in attendance and the new ones . . . not equal to them."[1]

Although Buchanan was not a member of any church, he instructed his niece: "Be constant in your devotion to God. . . . Men are short-sighted and know not the consequence of their own actions." His pessimism about human nature was unremitting. As he informed his niece in 1851, "The most brilliant prospects are often overcast, and those who commence life under favorable auspices are often unfortunate." During the 1840s he sent Harriet to one of the best-known girls' boarding schools in the United States: the Roman Catholic Convent School in Georgetown. Buchanan was not a Catholic, any more than he was a nativist. Still, he thought it best to warn his niece: "Your religious principles are doubtless so well-settled that you will not become a nun." There was little chance of that, for Harriet was a charming, social butterfly who enjoyed lengthy visits to friends.

Buchanan's letters to Harriet and all his family were the austere, distant expressions of a lifetime bachelor. He did not sign them with soft words of affection, once closing a letter to Harriet with the ponderous: "believe me to be yours with the highest consideration." Usually full of warnings about what not to do, in time he teased about her numerous boyfriends. Although he grudgingly accepted the reality that girls of Harriet's generation chose their own husbands, he extended unsolicited advice about her suitors. He advised her to avoid flattery, never to rush into marriage, and to pick a husband with "good moral habits" and enough money to keep her in the style to which she was accustomed. "Never engage yourself to any person without my previous advice." When a rich English earl twice her age proposed, he sternly warned against such a choice. Harriet, loyal and grateful to her uncle, followed his commandments, marrying—with Buchanan's approval—a wealthy Baltimore banker when she was thirty-seven years old.

In the meantime Harriet, along with a faithful housekeeper, Hetty Parker, ran Wheatland. In the spring of 1849 Buchanan dispatched his niece to Philadelphia to buy the heavy walnut furniture that soon filled the house. Buchanan organized his large study with its separate entrance on the east side of the house so that public men who called were kept away from the front parlors. Such a separation of spheres was a statement of the middle-class gentility that Buchanan had attained. In his study he found ample room for his desk and the new bookshelves he commissioned for his library. His books reflected his personality, for they were unmistakably the fare of a serious public man. He subscribed to the *Congressional Globe*, with its reports of the votes and speeches in the Senate and House. He had copies of the *Federalist Papers* and the debates over the formation of the U.S. Constitution and its ratification, along with Chancellor James Kent's *Commentaries*. He read Jared Sparks's laudatory biography of George Washington. Only a few novels by Charles Dickens and Sir Walter Scott's romances set in medieval Scotland, so popular with this generation of southerners, gave any indication that Buchanan ever read fiction.

Now that Lancaster had stagecoach and railroad connections to Baltimore and Philadelphia, Buchanan filled his time entertaining visitors. He chastised those who traveled through Pennsylvania on their way to Washington when they did not spend at least a night at Wheatland. To a fellow member of Polk's cabinet and his future secretary of the navy, Isaac Toucey, he lamented in June 1849 that he had not heard from any of Polk's cabinet, a group whose friendship a lonely bachelor intended to maintain: "As it is my sincere desire to keep the chain of friendship bright between us, I have determined to break the ice and open a correspondence with you."

Wheatland, now home for his nieces and nephews, made Buchanan a respectable family man of more assured masculinity. Dubbed "the Sage of Wheatland," he now carried a satisfying nickname appropriate for his age and experience. As a country residence, his estate associated him with values of permanence and stability and established his respectability, always somewhat problematic when, as a bachelor, he had lived in the unsavory quarters of boardinghouses in Washington.

After years of hard work, Buchanan at first reveled in his freedom from affairs of state. He had grown tired of the incessant duties of the secretary of state in an era when there were never enough clerks available to assist in the department's correspondence. Now he read, organized his garden, served as a host to overnight visitors who enjoyed his cigars and rye whiskey, wrote long letters, and spent some evenings in Lancaster's best-known tavern, the Grapes. He had time for carriage rides down the Marietta Pike, and never a man of great imagination, he celebrated the stereotypes of rural living—"a cozy time in the country" during the winter and in the spring, "the concerts of birds." To be sure, James Buchanan never removed himself entirely from either party politics or public issues. In fact he planned to edit and publish a volume of his speeches along with an autobiograpny—a "sketch of my life" that would display "what I have been and what I am."

Before he had time to do so, his political prospects improved. The presidential calendar for most aspirants— incumbent presidents were exceptions—began at least two years before an election, usually starting with solicitations of leaders from other states who might command delegations to national party conventions. Buchanan believed his chances were especially favorable in Virginia and Pennsylvania, states with large delegations. Naturally he disclaimed any interest in the nomination; in December 1851, he wrote, "The grand theatre of President making [in Washington] . . . is not my way." The reality was different. He traveled to Washington several times to meet with Democratic senators and representatives. He turned his attention to the schism in the Pennsylvania Democracy, vying with his rivals George Dallas and Senator Simon Cameron for control of the state party.

As was customary for nineteenth-century presidential aspirants, Buchanan presented his views to the public in letters. For years successful politicians like Henry Clay and Martin Van Buren had sent statements of their positions to influential newspaper editors and friends. In fact Buchanan's Harvest Home letter to a political rally in August 1847 had been just such a self-conscious "platform letter" intended to promote his chances in 1848. In it Buchanan had proposed the extension of the Missouri Compromise line prohibiting slavery north of 36° 30' (the southern boundary of Missouri) across the United States to the Pacific coast. Slavery would be prohibited north of the line, and south of it, as he explained, "the question was to be decided by the people." He did not specify when and how the people would do this, that is, at what phase in their territorial history, nor through what governing body. Harking back to a solution accepted by Congress and the country in 1820, Buchanan held, even as new territories were organized and added to the United States, that the "best security in the hour of danger is to cling fast to . . . time-honored principles."

Anticipating the 1852 presidential election, Buchanan wrote again on the issue in November 1850, this time in a letter to a public meeting in Philadelphia that took over three hours to read. This widely distributed "Letter to a Public Meeting" was the longest, most detailed, and most quoted

statement of Buchanan's views before his election to the presidency in 1856. The passage of the Compromise of 1850, one
of whose provisions was Congress's acceptance of California
as a free state, required a new statement. Following the position of many southerners, he abandoned the Missouri Compromise for the finality of this new legislation passed in 1850.
Exaggerating the "muttering thunder we hear from the
South," he applauded the defeat of the Wilmot Proviso, which
would have closed to slavery all territory incorporated into the
United States after the Mexican-American War.

To this technically antislavery Pennsylvanian who believed
that northerners must be mute on slavery and must join the
growing number of southern Democrats in a national party,
the Wilmot Proviso was only another example of "the spirit
of fanaticism . . . in the ascendant . . . which placed the divisions of the Union in hostile array." Rather than help free
slaves, antislavery agitation held up the process and "deprived
the slave of many privileges which he formerly enjoyed,
because of the stern necessity thus imposed upon the master
to provide for his personal safety and that of his family." It was
a theme to which Buchanan would return in his inaugural
address in 1857.

Distaste for antislavery northerners—for those who would
change the ancient bargain of the U.S. Constitution—permeated
Buchanan's approach to the growing differences between the
two sections. It emerged not only from his party affiliation and
his personality, but from his residence in Pennsylvania. From
its beginnings his native state had harbored Quakers who, as
Buchanan knew well from his years in the House and Senate,
had constantly petitioned Congress to end slavery. During the
1820s the Pennsylvania legislature had passed "personal liberty"

laws intended to protect free Negroes and fugitive slaves from slave hunters. Given its location astride the Mason-Dixon Line separating slaveholding Maryland from the free states in the North, Pennsylvania was the center of a flourishing underground-railroad system.

The repugnance of some Pennsylvania citizens to slave hunting was evident in a violent encounter between a Maryland slave owner, Edward Gorsuch, intent on reclaiming his human property, and the protectors of his slaves located in a town in southern Pennsylvania. In 1851 the Christiana Riot erupted fifteen miles southeast of Buchanan's home in Lancaster when he was in residence. It ended with the death of Gorsuch and his son at the hands of a militant antislavery group that included free blacks. Buchanan thought the outcome outrageous. While local leaders opposing the return of fugitives envisioned the future in similar actions, Buchanan considered them fanatics who would destroy the Union.

Accordingly he vigorously supported the new version of the fugitive slave law in the Compromise of 1850. Yet few laws could have been better designed to infuriate northerners and remind otherwise apathetic citizens of the differences between the North and South than the rewriting of the 1793 fugitive slave law. According to the Compromise of 1850, owners tracking down alleged fugitives in the North were permitted to seize them without due process. Federal marshals, not, as in the past, state judges, received larger payments if fugitives were returned to slavery than if they were freed. The final version of the fugitive slave law established penalties for anyone helping a slave escape. Instead "good citizens" must assist in the execution of the law, and given the necessity, Buchanan would doubtless have done his duty, returning slaves to masters in the name of the Union whose "benefits and blessings are inestimable. . . . God forbid that fanaticism should ever apply a torch to this, the grandest and most glorious temple which has ever been erected to political freedom on the face of the earth!" he wrote in November 1850.

By the spring of 1852, when Democrats would nominate a contender for the presidential election in the fall, Buchanan had joined Michigan's Senator Lewis Cass, the party's losing candidate in the 1848 election and, like Buchanan, a northern man with southern principles; Stephen Douglas, the Illinois senator; and William Marcy, a former governor of New York, as leading candidates. Theirs were the names that Democratic newspapers placed in large print on their mastheads, a crucial means of publicity. In a disappointing portent for Buchanan, despite his desire for a "harmonious" delegation, thirty-three delegates at the state convention in Harrisburg in March signed a protest against his nomination. Some did so because they supported Simon Cameron's faction, a group who had few policy differences with Buchanan but simply preferred Cameron. Others, followers of David Wilmot, the Pennsylvania congressman who had authored the Wilmot Proviso, could not swallow Buchanan's concessions to the South.

As always, Buchanan denied his intentions, though few aspirants did more than he to gain the nomination. However, he had often been disappointed in his presidential ambitions, and age had tamped down some of his political yearnings. Now he repeated in several letters in the spring of 1852, "If success attends me, very well; if not, defeat will cost me neither 'a night's rest nor a meal's victuals.' Thank heaven! I know how to be happy in retirement."

Yet he had hopes, if not expectations, and so continued to

write letters, travel to Richmond and Washington, and meet with influential party men at Wheatland. A clever politician, he advised his circle of correspondents to think twice about nominating Cass, his principal competitor, because, according to Buchanan, the Michigan senator could not carry Pennsylvania, with its twenty-seven electoral votes. Gradually Buchanan came to think that his prospects were improving, mostly because of his southern support. William King of Alabama, his friend from his congressional days, advised on the eve of the convention that if the South "adhered" to Buchanan, which he did not doubt it would, then the Pennsylvanian would be nominated.

Buchanan became known as a "doughface," a man whose principles did not conform to those of his section, but rather were malleable like dough. He was a northern man who favored the South. In time southern radicals would advance the position that Congress must protect slavery in all the territories before statehood, but at this point most still held to the clichés of midcentury conservatism that Buchanan had promoted in his 1850 letter: the sovereignty of the states and the "sacred" observance of their reserved rights, even to the point of accepting the right of state legislatures to negate federal legislation (the new fugitive slave law favoring the South was a specific exception that could not be overturned by states); a strict construction of the Constitution; resistance to the growth and increased spending of the federal government; and opposition to "the gradual absorption of unconstitutional power by the President & Congress." At the core of these abstractions rested Buchanan's leave-alone strategies to contain "the distractions of slavery" aggravating the South. But as he would soon find out, the absorption of new territory made keeping the status quo impossible.

When the six hundred Democratic delegates convened in Baltimore in June (many states gave delegates fractional votes so that the convention vote came to only 282), neither Buchanan nor Cass reached the two-thirds threshold required for nomination. The high bar established to protect southern interests made it increasingly difficult to nominate a candidate. In the beginning Buchanan's support was solid in states like Georgia, Alabama, and, for a time, Virginia. But he could never attract enough delegates from border or northern states. Instead Franklin Pierce of New Hampshire, an authentic "dark horse" in the traditional racetrack imagery of politics, finally won the Democratic nomination on the forty-ninth ballot. Anticipating his defeat and without "a single pang," Buchanan said a premature farewell to American politics. "After a long and stormy public life, I shall go into retirement without regret, and with a perfect consciousness that I have done my duty faithfully to my country in all the public circumstances in which I have been placed. . . . I only mean that I shall never hold another office."[2]

He declined the vice presidency and instead successfully supported his friend William King of Alabama for the position. Ever the public man who rarely shared private disappointments, he professed concern for his state, which in terms of its size and population deserved a president and still did not have one.

Six months after Franklin Pierce won the presidency with over 80 percent of the electoral vote, Buchanan returned to public life, this time as minister to Great Britain. (There were no ambassadors in the United States until 1893 because of the widespread sentiment that the rank and title were too monarchical.) Certainly the appointment was a demotion; he had

JEAN H. BAKER

already served as secretary of state. But even at sixty-one, he could never resist public life for long, and so in the name of duty, he accepted Pierce's call to service, never acknowledging the personal gratifications that made him accept: his interest in foreign policy, his boredom in retirement, and his desire to stay in the public eye.

Having initially accepted Pierce's offer in March 1853, Buchanan changed his mind and withdrew, not once but twice, only to finally accept the appointment. Later he felt it necessary to explain his vacillation. He gave as his reasons the administration's uncertainty about whether various issues would be negotiated by Secretary of State Marcy in Washington or by him in London, his own desire that his nomination not be counted against Pennsylvania's patronage appointments, and his reluctance to embarrass President Pierce by withdrawing after he had accepted. Actually his indecision, so similar to his course over his appointment to the Supreme Court, was characteristic—the result of having no audience before which to rehearse his private choices. In fact Buchanan rarely hesitated over public policies. But to his detractors he again seemed to display the ways of a frivolous female. Secretary of State Marcy concluded that "the truth is old bachelors as well as young maids do not always know their own minds. But if he ever meant to go he can assign no sufficient cause for changing his mind." Finally in the summer of 1853 Buchanan set sail for England, where he would serve as minister for nearly three years.[3]

James Buchanan was an efficient, hardworking, and exceedingly well-informed foreign minister during an important period in Anglo-American affairs. As a veteran of the Polk cabinet who had enthusiastically pursued expansionist policies in

Oregon and Mexico, Buchanan now faced a related issue of concern to the Pierce administration: the refusal of the British to withdraw from several islands off the coast of Honduras and to stop meddling in Nicaragua, where the recent Clayton-Bulwer Treaty had established a commitment to joint Anglo-American control of any future canal. At stake was the Monroe Doctrine, the backbone of American foreign policy at the time, which prohibited European powers from meddling in the Western Hemisphere. Polk had expanded the doctrine, reaffirming Monroe's noncolonization clause (with Canada an exception) and maintaining that the United States found unacceptable interference or "domination" by Europeans in its ever-expanding part of the world. Of course the doctrine held no international standing but was simply a statement of the American desire to have supreme authority everywhere in the Western Hemisphere. Only national pride and the growing power of the United States sustained Polk's statement.

In late September 1853 Buchanan had the first of over 150 meetings with the English foreign minister, Lord Clarendon. For the next three years these two men met in Clarendon's office, mostly amicably, to discuss what Buchanan considered the most aggravating question between Great Britain and the United States: the British presence in Central America. Throughout, Clarendon was busy with other matters—especially the Crimean War, in which France, Turkey, and Great Britain fought against Russia. Because it began in the spring of 1854, the conflict often interfered with Buchanan's access to key English officials. Sometimes a lonely Buchanan, who enjoyed his discussions with Clarendon, asked for a meeting even when there was no important business to discuss.

Before his first audience with Clarendon, Buchanan had

been busy searching for a place to live and work in a city he thought "horribly expensive," finally finding a house at 56 Hartley Street on Cavendish Square where he could combine the two. He had chosen as the secretary of the legation the wealthy, newly married Daniel Sickles, whom he expected would enjoy his honeymoon in England. Buchanan anticipated that the new Mrs. Sickles, a woman he found "both handsome and agreeable," would soon provide a female touch to the ministry. But instead Sickles brought his mistress to England and left his pregnant wife, Teresa, at home. (Later during Buchanan's presidency the flamboyant Sickles murdered his wife's lover, Philip Barton Key, and Washington gossips held that Buchanan visited him in jail before Sickles's successful defense of temporary insanity over his wife's adultery.) Of greater significance than Sickles's philandering was the new secretary of the legation's irresponsibility about his duties, for he preferred the social scene in London to serving as a clerk. Worst of all, his handwriting, so critical in a secretary, was illegible, and often an assistant clerk had to recopy his dispatches.

Buchanan's first diplomatic crisis involved not Central America or even where the English could fish off New England, but clothes. Shortly after his arrival he had been informally presented to Queen Victoria, and a few months later she invited him to dinner. He found her gracious and dignified, yet, as he informed Harriet, without many "personal charms." But when Secretary of State Marcy's circular on court dress arrived directing all diplomats abroad to wear the simple dress of an American citizen, Buchanan's social life, so critical to the success of any diplomatic mission, but especially that in England, was jeopardized. In simple American dress, according to a British protocol officer, he could not attend the court or the opening of Parliament. Nor was the plain outfit of an American suitable for entrance into the dining rooms and salons of the court or the gentry, where a clever diplomat circulated with his ears open, listening to off-the-record news and gossip. In the spring, caught between diplomatic orders over what he should wear and the insistence of the British that all diplomats appear in full "court dress," Buchanan caused a stir by staying home from the opening of Parliament.

By the time Queen Victoria asked him again for dinner, Buchanan had made up his mind. He would not adorn himself with the gold and embroidery, lace and jewelry, or even the patent leather boots worn by some envoys. Rather he embellished the simple dress of an American citizen with a black-handled and hilted sword, considered on both sides of the Atlantic the mark of a gentleman. At least he would not be mistaken for a servant, an embarrassment that had already occurred. As he explained to Harriet, he appeared in the kind of outfit that he had always worn at presidential parties in Washington—"a black coat, white waist coat & cravat & black pantaloons & dress boots, with the addition of a very plain black handled and black hilted sword." The *London Herald* was disgusted with this violation of dress codes, referring to Buchanan as "the gentleman in the black coat from Yankeeland."

The reaction at home was more positive, as the great dress affair, over which he had agonized so long, redounded to Buchanan's advantage, and a man who was stiff and prim was transformed in the newspapers into a common fellow. Few episodes in the period so strikingly differentiated what Americans considered their democracy of the people from the snobbery of the English class system. Twisting the tail of the British lion had long been a popular American sport, and the fact that one of the nation's diplomats had successfully challenged the foppish customs of the English earned Buchanan the respect of many Americans. Newspapers in the United States praised his refusal to dress like an aristocrat. The *Pennsylvania Patriot* called him a "true man—a republican in fact and truth." A friend from Pennsylvania, predicting that Buchanan would now be the Democratic candidate in 1856, wrote that this insignificant matter of dress had impressed "the masses of the people, of all parties."[4]

By the end of 1853 Buchanan and Clarendon had established a routine for their weekly conferences. From his lessons in Russia in the 1830s, Buchanan knew that the diplomatic wheel turned slowly and that agreements between sovereign states took patience and persistence. For the next two years, with occasional asides to discuss the Crimean War, their discourse encompassed the violation of American neutrality by the English minister in Washington, who was illegally recruiting soldiers for the British army, the British meddling in Central America along with the naval squadron sent to the West Indies, and Buchanan's preoccupation with Cuba. Most discussions were friendly, but there were exceptions. On one occasion Clarendon seized Buchanan by the lapels and shook him, and the English minister sometimes disparaged the American behind his back as "the Old Buck . . . a crafty sinner . . . as proud as Lucifer." Ever the professional, Buchanan kept private his personal assessments of English diplomats.

For Buchanan, Clarendon's agreement to a treaty was the necessary step toward implementing his instructions of getting the British to abandon what the Pierce administration considered their defiance of the Polk doctrine in Central America. Buchanan precisely followed his instructions from the president and the secretary of state. These were threefold: first, to persuade the English to abandon the Bay Islands (off the northeast coast of Honduras), which the British had seized in 1841 and which rightly, according to the Americans, belonged to Honduras; second, to force the British out of mahogany-rich Belize, where they had encroached after originally having no more than log-cutting concessions from the Spanish; and third, to end the British protectorate over the Mosquito Indians, considered by the Americans no more than a ruse for English control of Greytown, an important station at the mouth of the San Juan River on the Caribbean side of Nicaragua. Greytown had particular significance because it was astride a potential isthmian canal route. What Buchanan did not volunteer was information about a recently established American land and mining company, which held a dubious patent to the region inhabited by the Mosquito Indians.

In the beginning Clarendon was ignorant of the specifics of these tiny colonies in Central America. The British, as he informed Buchanan, presided over a large empire and were currently at war with the Russians in the Crimea. When Buchanan exaggerated that the Bay Island of Ruatan was one of the "most commanding positions in the world," Clarendon replied that he had hardly heard of the tiny island whose British control so aggravated the American minister. The carefully prepared Buchanan often found himself giving the British minister a geography lesson. When Buchanan noted that "our good mother has been all the time engaged, for one hundred & fifty years in annexing one possession after another

[but] raises her hands with holy horror if the daughter annexed territories adjacent to herself, " Clarendon joked that the United States was "a chip off the old block." The latter response gave Buchanan the opportunity to argue the enduring reality of nineteenth- and twentieth-century Anglo-American relations—that there was no reason for England to object. "We extended the English language, Christianity, liberty, & law wherever we went upon our own continent & converted uninhabited regions into civilized communities, from the trade with which they derived great advantages."[5]

During some of his conferences with Clarendon, Buchanan turned the conversation to his special preoccupation—Cuba. By this time the American minister believed that the key to purchasing the Spanish possession lay in persuading international bondholders, whose investments in Spain were threatened by that nation's uncertain economy, to pressure the government to sell Cuba to the United States in order to pay its creditors. But such a change would require delicate diplomatic discussions with Great Britain and France. By the summer of 1854 Buchanan believed Clarendon was ready to bring British pressure on the Spanish to sell the island.

That summer Buchanan received new instructions from Washington with regard to Cuba. He must travel to Paris and meet with other American diplomats "to adopt measures for perfect concert of action" with regard to purchasing the Spanish possession. Buchanan complained to Pierce on September 1, 1854, "It is impossible for me to devise any other plan for the acquisition of Cuba than what I already have presented to you. We are willing to purchase and our object is to induce them to sell." There was no need for a meeting. But the president was insistent. And so began the Ostend Manifesto, so-called because the statement written by the three American ministers—Buchanan; Pierre Soulé, the hotheaded minister in Spain who believed nothing could save Cuba from America's "mighty grasp"; and John Mason, who served in France—was issued from the small town in Belgium. Eventually what the three ministers called a report became known as a manifesto, forever linked to Buchanan's name.

Most likely James Buchanan wrote the report; certainly it bears some of his phrases and style. Although his defenders argue that he was a reluctant participant and that he toned down Soulé's aggressive language, he signed a document that represented one of the high-water marks of nineteenth-century expansionism. Buchanan justified the purchase of the island for $100 million on the grounds that Cuba was a natural geographic appendage of the United States. According to the three ministers, taking Cuba was a matter of self-preservation for the United States. Given the island's location commanding the mouth of the Mississippi, "it belongs naturally to that great family of States of which the Union is the Providential Nursery. . . . If after offering Spain a fair price for Cuba far beyond its present value and this shall have been refused . . . by every law human and Divine we shall be justified in wresting it from Spain."

The document absolved the United States of any blame if force was used. It further claimed, in a considerable stretch by the ministers, that the United States had never acquired "a foot of territory except by fair purchase." No doubt Buchanan crafted the homely, metaphorical vindication that forcefully taking Cuba was similar in principle to the natural law that an individual is justified "in tearing down the burning house of his neighbor, if there were no other means of preventing the flames from destroying his own home." The reference, of course, was to Buchanan's and the South's exaggerated fear that a slave rebellion might break out in Cuba, imperiling slavery in the United States.

The Ostend Manifesto arrived in Washington during a period of great volatility. Throughout the year Congress had argued Stephen Douglas's plan to organize the territories of Kansas and Nebraska. A bill had finally passed in May 1854, embracing Douglas's doctrine of popular sovereignty. The idea was that local residents, before the assembling of a state constitutional convention that would have the final determination, might decide questions relating to slavery in their early life as a territory. Such a law explicitly repealed the Missouri Compromise, because it meant that slaveholders who had been intimidated from taking slaves into land from which slavery would ultimately be prohibited now were free to take slaves into any territory. With the stakes so high, the Kansas-Nebraska Act led to furious debates between Whigs and Democrats as well as between northerners and southerners.

Southerners applauded the Ostend Manifesto and Buchanan's role in it. They believed, as did Buchanan, that given its location, Cuba, still a haven for slave traders, might also produce a slave uprising, the mechanism by which the entire United States might erupt in what this generation called "servile rebellions." As such reasoning went, instability in Cuba threatened the security of slavery in the United States. Even without the image of falling dominoes—from slaves fighting for freedom in Cuba to those on the mainland rebelling against their masters—southerners considered Cuba natural slave territory. There was economic potential as well, far more so than in the American Southwest. Cuba had prosperous sugar plantations, not deserts like New Mexico and Arizona.

On the other hand, northerners saw in the Ostend Manifesto and southern reaction to it another example of an aggressive slaveocracy intent on dominating the federal government and extending the ownership of black Americans into new territories. Southerners were increasingly seen in the North as a minority imposing their society and values on the rest of the United States. When enemies of the administration publicized the document, Pierce, properly embarrassed by the uproar, downplayed his ministers' report. Secretary of State Marcy, ambitious for a Democratic nomination in 1856 that would require northern support beyond his home state of New York, eventually repudiated the document. Instead, for the rest of his life, Buchanan smelled of the Ostend Manifesto, which according to the beholder was either a stink or a perfume.

By 1855 James Buchanan was ready to come home. But Pierce refused to appoint a successor and asked him "to see it through" after the British sent a fleet to the Caribbean. So he stayed, complaining in the fall of 1854 that his labors were "like those of a drayman. Have you no bowels?" As a minister, he had been successful in diminishing British power in Honduras and Nicaragua, and certainly he had made the English more cognizant of American intentions in the Caribbean and Central America.

With Pierce's reputation declining and his promise not to seek another nomination, Buchanan was moving onstage to become the best available man for the 1856 Democratic nomination. Typically he disclaimed any interest, writing a friend on February 20, 1856: "In the beginning I did all I could to prevent any movement in my favor & what has since been done has been entirely spontaneous, at least so far as I am personally concerned. I had hoped and believed that my public life would terminate with my present mission, but events must now take their course at the Cincinnati Convention." Meanwhile the "Buchaneers" saluted his integrity, his ability, and his experience, and if some timid northern Democrats believed him contaminated by the Ostend Manifesto, Buchanan nevertheless benefited from his absence from the United States during the disputes over the Kansas-Nebraska Act.

Despite what he said, no one doubted that Buchanan could be drafted, and as was his habit, he soon was openly stalking the nomination, while denying any interest in it. Even before he left England he arranged a dinner with a Catholic archbishop, during which he diplomatically praised the head of the American Catholic Church, Archbishop John Hughes. Buchanan's compliments flew across the Atlantic, and Hughes was soon using his prestige to persuade well-placed Catholics to support Buchanan. A few weeks before he left London in February 1856 for a vacation on the continent, Buchanan acknowledged to Marcy, albeit in the third person, that he was ambivalent about the presidency. And he accurately predicted that the challenges of the next president would be as great as any ever faced by an American president. "No competent and patriotic man to whom it may be offered should shrink from the responsibility, yet he may well accept it as the greatest trial of his life."

Buchanan arrived in New York one day after he celebrated, no doubt with a cigar and several glasses of Madeira, his sixty-fifth birthday aboard the steamer *Arago*. A month earlier Pennsylvania Democrats had given him what they had denied him so many times in the past: their unanimous support. Amid much acclaim on his arrival, he received visitors at the Astor House in New York and appeared at a reception at City Hall. In Philadelphia and Lancaster exuberant receptions with bands, fireworks, and a cannon named "Old Buck" cheered James Buchanan, the Democratic party's man of the hour.

Against the backdrop of two sensational events in May 1856—the beating into unconsciousness of the Massachusetts senator Charles Sumner by a South Carolina congressman and the retaliatory raid of the abolitionist John Brown against a proslavery settlement that had earlier killed six antislavery Kansas settlers—Democratic delegates met in Cincinnati to nominate a candidate for president. The first order of business was to write a platform. The final version read as if James Buchanan had written it himself. It called for a federal government of limited powers, vigorous support of the fugitive slave law, upholding "the domestic institutions of the states," an end to antislavery (though not proslavery) agitation, and "proper efforts to assure [U.S.] ascendancy in the Gulf of Mexico."

The incumbent, Franklin Pierce, hoped for the nomination, despite growing criticism of his administration and its policies in Kansas and despite his earlier promise not to seek a second term. So, too, did the ambitious Stephen Douglas, the best known of Democratic policy makers whose Kansas-Nebraska Act had voided the Missouri Compromise and opened the West to endless fights over slavery. As principal architect of the doctrine of "popular sovereignty," Douglas received considerable southern support. Lewis Cass, the defeated Democratic candidate in 1848, was also a contender. But Buchanan's managers controlled the convention machinery, and throughout the convention a triumvirate of U.S. senators—John

Slidell of Louisiana, Jesse Bright of Indiana, and Thomas Bayard of Delaware—effectively lobbied for the man whom they presented as a well-seasoned leader from a state between North and South with the second largest number of electoral votes in the nation.

In the early ballots Douglas and Pierce, Buchanan's principal challengers, alternated with each other in order to prevent Buchanan from getting the necessary two-thirds. Pierce went first, but even with Douglas's delegates the president never had more votes than Buchanan. Pierce's delegates then shifted to Douglas. But Buchanan's support held up; Douglas withdrew, and on the eighteenth ballot James Buchanan received the nomination, the first step toward the prize he had so long sought. To balance the selection of a nominee from a free state (though given Buchanan's views this was not needed), the popular John Breckinridge, a congressman from the slave state of Kentucky, was chosen as vice president.

There were two other candidates in the 1856 presidential election: Millard Fillmore, the former president who ran on the Know-Nothings' anti-Catholic and anti-immigrant platform; and John C. Frémont, representing the rapidly growing Republicans. The Know-Nothings were this generation's political phenomenon. The American party was their official name, and their platform advocated the extension of the naturalization period to twenty-one years. "Americans to rule America" became their pledge. The nominee of the Republicans had no political experience. But as an explorer and military man, the forty-three-year-old Frémont had name recognition and youth. The first Republican presidential candidate in history, he stood for a political organization dedicated to prohibiting slavery in the territories, but not interfering with slavery in the states where it already existed. If Frémont represented the vigor of the Republic and an implicit challenge to the archaic system of slavery, at least in the territories, then Buchanan stood as the experienced captain who might steady the ship of state in stormy times. Buchanan's opponents saw him differently: they satirized him in political cartoons as a fussy old man and dressed him in women's clothes.

Buchanan did not campaign; such entreaties by the candidate himself were considered violations of the national understanding that conferring public office was a gift of the people. He did write letters, and in the speech he gave to a committee notifying him of his nomination, Buchanan pledged himself to run on the Democratic platform—nothing more, nothing less. Buchanan had always believed popular sovereignty potentially disruptive. But as an obedient Democrat, he surrendered his personal views, supporting "the right of the people of all the territories to form a constitution with or without slavery." However, he could never abandon his pessimism, nor his view that he was somehow above the crass necessities of soliciting votes. But as he had described presidential contenders in December of 1851, "The wisest and most sagacious men become dunces when seized by a desire for the presidency." Still, he considered his election the only means to save the Union, and as he famously wrote, he did not want to survive the Union. To a Pennsylvania Democrat, Buchanan explained in the summer of 1856, "The Union is in danger and the people everywhere begin to know it. Black Republicans must be, as they can be with justice, boldly assailed as disunionists and this charge must be reiterated again and again."

His political friends campaigned vigorously, hastening to New York at a critical point in the summer of 1856 to raise money from wealthy New Yorkers. There was even talk that the rich candidate had helped to finance his own campaign. Buchanan's task was to carry the South and take some northern states, especially the great catch of Pennsylvania. Yet there was apprehension even in his home state, where Frémont was popular.

In September, when state elections in Maine revealed the strength of the Republicans, Buchanan was surprised but did not take seriously a political organization he believed would soon disappear. To hold California, he endorsed the building of a railroad to the Pacific, a lapse from the Democrats' stance against federally funded internal improvements, but one that had been accepted in the platform. Buchanan justified the railroad as having a military purpose "for safe and speedy communication between the Atlantic and Pacific coasts" and therefore falling under the constitutional power to declare war and repel invasions.

On Election Day, 79 percent of the all-male and overwhelmingly white electorate went to the polls, the fourth highest turnout in American presidential voting. In one of those rare elections in which party allegiances are reshuffled, Buchanan carried every slaveholding state except for Maryland as well as five northern states including Pennsylvania. In all he received 45 percent of the total vote to Frémont's 33 and Fillmore's 22, and he carried nineteen states and 174 electoral votes to Frémont's 114 and Fillmore's 8. In a victory speech from his porch at Wheatland, the newly elected president voiced familiar themes: "The people of the North" (meaning those who had voted for the Republicans) had forgotten the warning of the Founding Fathers about "geographical parties." They had supported a "dangerous party"; they had attacked southerners, while "the southern people still cherish a love for the Union."

Buchanan had long since chosen sides. Both physically and politically, he had only one farsighted eye, and it looked southward. Looking to the past and heralding the Democratic party's eternal principles against the "isms" of free-soilism and antislaveryism, the president-elect was blind to what was happening in the North. Even in his home state the combined Frémont-Fillmore vote was only a few hundred less than his, and he a favorite son. Democrats lost eleven of sixteen free states to an unknown party with a candidate who had never held public office. In fact elated Republicans labeled the election a "victorious defeat." Ominously for Democrats, turnouts in the North increased by 7 percent over 1852, and most of these new voters were Republicans. But Buchanan, despite his experience in politics, read the opposition party as ephemeral as lightning bugs in August.

In his desire to end division between the North and South, the president-elect moved beyond the tradition of permissible institutionalized antagonism between political organizations. The concept of the loyal opposition, inherited from Great Britain, sanctioned criticism of administrations and the presentation of alternative policies. What it did not permit was the castigation of another party as disloyal and un-American, as Buchanan held the Republicans. In his years as president, Buchanan did a great deal to popularize the view that the Republicans were a threat to the South, thereby encouraging its secession from the Union when Abraham Lincoln was elected president in 1860.

Nor did Buchanan recognize the growing power of antislaveryism. Instead, complimenting his home state on its

Democratic vote, the president-elect serenely announced that Pennsylvania had "breasted the storm and [driven] it back. The night is departing, and the roseate and propitious morn now breaking upon us promises a long day of peace and prosperity for our country. To secure this all we of the North have to do is to permit our Southern neighbors to manage their own domestic affairs, as they permit us to manage ours."

Besides his pronounced prosouthernism, Buchanan's personality also damaged his prospects for a successful presidency. He had always been a cautious pessimist, lacking the ebullience that so often undergirds the boldness of good presidents. In the biblical phrase he had been repeating all his life, "Sufficient unto the day is the evil thereof." He had never been certain whether it was worth it to be a Supreme Court justice or minister to England or secretary of state. Of course he had always wanted to be president, but the presidency had not come when he'd wished. "The things we desire do not arrive or if they do come it is not in the terms or manner which gives us the most pleasure," he wrote a friend, quoting La Rochefoucauld. He remembered as well a similarly grim verse that fitted his view of life: "Will fortune never come with both hands full? / She either gives a stomach and no food, / Or else a feast and takes away the stomach."[6]

3

The Buchanan Presidency—
Theory and Practice

When James Buchanan took the presidential oath of office in March 1857, he knew more about the American presidency than anyone in the United States. For more than thirty-five years he had observed chief executives in action, having had some contact with every one of the ten presidents from James Monroe to Franklin Pierce. At first he had watched from afar as an impressionable young congressman and then with growing experience and seniority as a senator, cabinet officer, leader of the Democratic party, and most recently as Pierce's foreign minister to Great Britain. He had been the subordinate of some and a friend, though not an intimate one, of both Polk and Pierce.

And of course for many years he had wanted to be president, at least until he actually won the office. At a time in American history when presidents downgraded their roles to that of administrators, and rarely acknowledged themselves as initiators of policy, Buchanan had developed an unusual perspective. Influenced by two strong chief executives—Jackson and Polk— he had come to appreciate the possibilities of the presidency as an office of power. Yet, as an admirer of the Constitution, he dutifully praised the separation of executive authority from that of Congress and the Supreme Court.

In his writings on the presidency, Buchanan insisted that the office must never be held by a professional military man, arriving at this conclusion when one of his partisan enemies, General Winfield Scott, became the Whig candidate for president in 1852. Military men, according to Buchanan, expected to have their orders obeyed and would naturally expand their prerogatives too far. Their training differed from that of civilians, and they especially lacked the instinct to consider opposing opinions and negotiate compromises. Nor did they have expert knowledge of the Constitution and the laws. Instead Buchanan saw the presidency as the preserve of lawyers, with Andrew Jackson and George Washington possible exceptions, though neither were professional soldiers and Jackson had studied law. Washington, the hero of Buchanan and every American, was a leader summoned from Mount Vernon by the people during an emergency, in the mold of the Roman hero Cincinnatus. Buchanan knew that political parties made the spontaneity that had called both men to service impossible in his generation, but he believed that he had not sought, but rather had been chosen, in similar fashion, by the people. Such an interpretation facilitated an expansive view of the president's powers.

From Buchanan's perspective, the demands of the office required a man of calm and firm temperament, a commanding leader, as he wrote in 1852, who was neither jealous of his powers nor "irritable and quarrelsome" in his personality. A president must be a loyal party man, as Buchanan knew himself to be when he dutifully supported the Democratic candidates after his disappointments in 1844, 1848, and 1852. Presidents must also be experienced public officials, familiar with the issues, and forthcoming, never secretive or devious, in their opinions on public matters. They should appoint a harmonious, unified cabinet, a consideration that Andrew Jackson, for all his political talents, had not recognized. As a result Jackson had suffered from a collection of contentious department heads, supplemented by an unofficial group of advisers dubbed his kitchen cabinet. Buchanan intended to make no such mistake.

At a time when Whigs publicly challenged the presidential veto as granting the president too much authority, Buchanan considered the veto the least dangerous of presidential powers. Rather, a despotic presidency might emerge from the president's control over the departments, his power to influence public opinion, and his authority as commander in chief. Still, Buchanan believed overturning congressional legislation was an authority to be used sparingly, and then only from a deep conviction that the people supported his position. On the other hand, Buchanan considered the powers of both president and Congress restricted because they had emerged as a grant from a higher authority—the people's delegation of their authority to the sovereign states. But the president had clear authority over foreign policy, an area in which Buchanan had specialized. Overall, "a strict construction of the powers of the government is the only true as well as the only safe theory of the Constitution," said Buchanan, expressing a view familiar to all Americans, but especially embraced by southerners.[1]

Buchanan was describing not only his philosophy of government but, in his comments about the temperament of an ideal president, his view of himself. As he took office and applied his presidential formulas, his performance as the fifteenth president of the United States represented not that of the traditional weak executive of the pre–Civil War period, but rather that of a strong, if exceptionally misguided, one. He might write of strict construction, but if the South's interests were at stake, he would extend the authority of the executive—what Alexander Hamilton once described as the presidency's "competent powers"—to that section's protection. In this sense he would be, in a phrase of Polk's, president *himself.*

Weeks before his inauguration Buchanan began the task of creating a consensual cabinet that he anticipated would serve as a sounding board for his ideas. Bombarded by suggestions from political leaders throughout the country, he informed a friend that he would pick his own cabinet. For a lonely man, its members must be friends, who would fill his days with conversation, share his dinners, and, as later transpired, when their wives were out of town, sleep in the White House. For six weeks in 1861, when chaos overtook the Buchanan White House, his newly appointed secretary of the Treasury, John Dix, slept there at the president's insistence. Dix soon discovered that a distraught Buchanan liked to come to his room late at night to discuss, with the president doing most of the talking, the disintegration of the United States.

Given the use of cabinet appointments to fulfill all kinds of party, sectional, and personal considerations, the initial task of choosing its members proved as complicated as a difficult crossword puzzle. Mostly Buchanan stayed in Wheatland as he worked on his cabinet selections and his inaugural address, but in late January he traveled to Washington.

This journey proved to be a mistake, for he contracted a debilitating dysentery, called the National Hotel disease, which was the result of frozen pipes spilling fecal matter into the hotel's kitchen and cooking water. Several guests died, including Buchanan's nephew and Harriet Lane's brother,

Eskridge Lane, who was serving as his secretary at the time. Buchanan survived but was intermittently afflicted for months with severe vomiting, cramps, and diarrhea. Even in March, during a periodic flare-up, he worried that he might faint or worse during his inaugural speech, and so a doctor sat in the front row, handy with brandy and smelling salts. For the pessimistic Buchanan, his own suffering at the moment of this supreme triumph enacted his fatalistic notions that disappointment and tragedy inevitably followed success.

In the end Buchanan's cabinet selections proved a disaster. To choose, as he did, four members from the future Confederacy and three northern Democrats who, like Buchanan, were doughfaces was an insult to the North. All four of the southerners had at one time or another been large slaveholders, and his special pet, Secretary of the Treasury Howell Cobb of Georgia, had once owned over one thousand slaves. All were wealthy men—aristocratic southern politicos whom he enjoyed entertaining in the White House.

Only one of the cabinet's seven members—the lugubrious seventy-five-year-old Lewis Cass of Michigan, who purchased a new brown wig for the inauguration—came from west of the Appalachians, and Cass would be overshadowed by the president, who anticipated serving as his own secretary of state. Traditionally that officer served as an informal head of the cabinet but, again illustrating his perspective on the presidency, Buchanan wanted no firm alternative voice. He expected to concentrate on foreign policy, with the acquisition of Cuba a firm priority. Overall, the composition of Buchanan's cabinet revealed the incoming chief executive as no peacemaker but rather as a strong president intent on having his own way, surrounded by advisers who agreed with him. And for more than three and a half years there was acquiescence among his cabinet.

Buchanan did not acknowledge, much less reward, Stephen Douglas, the Illinois senator whose withdrawal as a candidate in the 1856 Democratic convention had made possible his own nomination. In a slap to free-soil Democrats, none of Douglas's inner circle of supporters was appointed to the cabinet or even to lesser jobs in the Post Office or in the Interior and State Departments. Actually Buchanan embarrassed Douglas, who worried about charges of nepotism when the president appointed Douglas's father-in-law, Madison Cutts, to a minor patronage position. Another man might have reached out to his opposition in such troubled times. But Buchanan chose no Republicans, though they represented a growing body of northern opinion that opposed the extension of slavery into the territories.

For Buchanan the Republican party was anathema. It would be his job to persuade northerners that Republicans were extremists who threatened the South with their antislavery propaganda. As he wrote a friend in December 1856, "The great object of my administration will be to arrest, if possible, the agitation of the Slavery question at the North and to destroy sectional parties," by which he meant the Republicans, not his own southern-leaning version of the Democrats. But by leaving out Republicans and even northern Democrats who were not so aggressively prosouthern as he, Buchanan dangerously isolated himself.

On that pleasant sunny March day in 1857, when James Buchanan took the oath of office, he was an imposing, vigorous figure, even at sixty-five. For Americans of the early nineteenth century, when the median age was nineteen, anyone over sixty was exceptional. Only 3 percent of white males lived so long, and longevity still conveyed wisdom. At least fifty pounds heavier than he had been in his twenties, the president's once blond hair had turned snow-white, the sure sign of a sagacious patriarch. Buchanan towered over Chief Justice Roger B. Taney when he bent his head to have a brief, and noteworthy, conversation with the latter before he took the oath of office.

For Buchanan his accession to the presidency, after so many years of dutiful service to men younger than he, brought relief. Rather than having to take orders from an inexperienced president like Pierce or a headstrong younger man like Polk, finally he was in charge. Faithful to a principle of Jacksonian Democrats and conscious of his age, he promised only one term. But his predecessor, Pierce, had made a similar commitment, and when the time came he had fiercely contested the 1856 nomination.

In his long inaugural address Buchanan called attention to the growing divisions in the Union over slavery in the territories and boldly offered his solution. First, Congress had no role in the decisions that individual territories made about slavery. It could neither sustain nor prohibit slavery in the territorial stage, as had been the case under the Missouri Compromise. Only the sovereign will of the people, when their delegates wrote a state constitution and they elected a legislature, could do so. Buchanan's pronouncement followed what had become at this point the moderate southern position, legislated by the Kansas-Nebraska Act of 1854—that individuals could settle in any territory with their slaves.

The argument, as it evolved during Buchanan's administration, focused on the point when agencies of government could legislate on slavery. Could territorial legislatures and conventions address the question at all? Must they remain mute until the territory had sufficient population to elect a constitutional convention prior to becoming a state? What exactly was the precise application of Stephen Douglas's doctrine of popular sovereignty? The Democratic platform of 1856 had hedged on this divisive issue. But increasingly southerners were pressing for the right of slave owners to take their human property into the territories and have it protected, at any time and in every place, even north of the Missouri Compromise line of 36° 30' latitude.

Some, like Senator Jefferson Davis of Mississippi, were going so far as to insist on a federal slave code. In their view, slavery followed the flag into the territories and must be safeguarded by the federal government. In a self-evident reversal these advocates of states' rights now proclaimed that the federal Congress must protect ownership of slaves. Buchanan, who cared little about slavery one way or the other, agreed with them in his inaugural address: "The sacred right of each individual [by which he meant white male citizens] must be preserved." Moreover, the agitation of northern fanatics had done no good, producing only "great evils to the master, the slave, and to the whole country."

Later Buchanan went further. In his third annual message to Congress in December 1859 (by this time he was a complete captive of the southern point of view), he promoted the view that black males were potential rapists and arsonists. The true defilers of what Buchanan called "the family altar," according to abolitionists, were white men who raped their female slaves. But in an official communication the president defended the anxiety of the South about slave rebellions, and, six weeks after John Brown's raid on Harpers Ferry, he offered a possible justification for secession: "If the peace of the domestic fireside throughout these states should ever be invaded, if mothers of families within this extensive region should not be able to rest at night without suffering dreadful apprehension of what may be their own fate and that of their children before morning, it would be vain to recount to such people the political benefits which result from the Union."

It was a theme he presented less explicitly in many of his messages. The South had the right to demand justice, he said, and that meant territories open to slavery for what Buchanan, using the southern vocabulary, called "a domestic institution," under the control of the states. And as part of this justice Buchanan included a rigorous enforcement of the fugitive slave law requiring the return of slaves from the North to their masters in the South. Besides, said Buchanan in his inaugural address, the question of popular sovereignty held "little practical importance." It lay within the jurisdiction of the judiciary, the third branch of the American government, in a case before the Supreme Court that would permanently settle the matter. Without referring by name to the Dred Scott case, Buchanan announced that he would "cheerfully submit" to the Court's ruling, no matter what it was.

The Dred Scott case had a long history before Buchanan referred to it in his inaugural address. It had begun in 1846 when the slave Dred Scott initially sued in the Missouri courts for his freedom on the basis that he had lived on free soil. His owner, an army doctor, had taken Scott with him when he was posted to Minnesota and Illinois. In the past courts had treated such suits inconsistently, often ruling that residence in a free territory conveyed freedom to slaves. In fact the Missouri circuit court had held that Scott was free by virtue of his residence in free territory. But the Missouri appeals court reversed the decision. Eventually, as Dred Scott's ownership and circumstances changed through death and inheritance, *Dred Scott v. Sandford* came into the federal courts. By 1856 it was a well-known judicial controversy with high-profile attorneys arguing both sides before the U.S. Supreme Court.

For Buchanan it seemed an opportunity to end forever the slave issue in the United States. And so, in early February as the nine members of the Court (five from slaveholding states) edged toward their decision, Buchanan and his friend Justice John Catron of Tennessee exchanged letters. Buchanan had originally asked about the status of the case, so that he might refer to it in his inaugural address. Catron responded that the justices were split, and that the new president should encourage his Pennsylvania friend Justice Robert Grier not to accept any limited judicial response but to seek a definitive solution. Only abolitionists like Frederick Douglass, William Lloyd Garrison, and John Brown, but certainly not mainstream Republicans, challenged slavery in the original states and in the nine slave states that had entered the United States after the ratification of the Constitution. So if the issue of slavery in the territories could be settled, the United States could move on to other matters. In Buchanan's view these would certainly involve the expansion of the United States southward into Mexico and Cuba, both ripe for slaveholding.

Following Catron's advice, a few weeks before his inauguration the president-elect wrote to Justice Grier, urging a comprehensive judgment that moved beyond the particulars of Dred Scott's individual status into that of all black Americans—slave and free, North and South. If a decision was reached, he wanted to use it as a launching point for a triumphant program of national harmony. Grier in turn promptly conferred with Chief Justice Roger Taney and Justice James Wayne of Georgia.

Eventually, after Buchanan's prodding, six justices including Grier and Catron made up the majority that, speaking through Taney, held slaves to be forever property and without any rights that white men were "bound" to protect. No black could be a citizen; hence Dred Scott could not sue for his freedom. The Missouri Compromise, with its congressional prohibition on slavery north of the 36° 30' line, was explicitly nullified. And as private property protected by the due process clause of the Fifth Amendment, slavery now could not be prohibited before statehood, even during the ambiguous stage of territorial status. The decision led Massachusetts senator Charles Sumner to wonder if there was a North left. By 1857 increasing numbers of free-soil and antislavery Americans believed that slavery was like southern kudzu vine. Once permitted into any area, it would grow everywhere, as slaveholders rushed into new territories with their human property.

When Buchanan took office, he already knew the outcome of the Dred Scott case. His comment that he would "cheerfully" submit to whatever the Court decided was, to say the least, disingenuous. More telling, he had been complicit in the decision, committing in his letters to Justices Catron and Grier the constitutional impropriety (or worse) of interfering with the Court's deliberations and violating his cherished separation of the judicial and executive branches. Republicans in the audience observed Taney and Buchanan whispering before the latter took the oath of office, and they believed the chief justice had advised Buchanan of what would be forthcoming two days later when the Supreme Court announced its decision. They concluded that the president had then inserted his comments. The truth was more damaging. Using his presidential authority, Buchanan had helped to frame the decision.

Without Buchanan's encouragement, Grier, the only northerner to join in Taney's final decision, might not have joined the others. Any ruling by five southern justices alone would have lacked the imprimatur of a national settlement. But with the Pennsylvanian's agreement, *Dred Scott* was nationalized. As one authority on the case, the historian Don Fehrenbacher, has concluded, "Buchanan's intervention contributed significantly to the change in the substance of the Dred Scott decision." Again, as with his choices for the cabinet, Buchanan extended the prerogatives of the presidency to promote southern interests and to grasp for the final solution of a problem that he believed was caused solely by interfering northerners. But rather than acknowledge that the Dred Scott decision destroyed their main platform, the Republicans, whom Buchanan felt should immediately "yield obedience," denounced and repudiated such an iniquitous judicial determination. Buchanan believed that the disruption of the Union that followed was their fault, not his.[2]

After his inauguration the new president concentrated on patronage appointments. A reluctant delegator of executive tasks forever absorbed in details, he spent hours, often at night, attired in dressing gown and slippers, unlit cigar in mouth, deciding on his choices, reviewing those as inconsequential as minor third- and fourth-class positions in the post office and even overriding cabinet members on some of their departmental choices. Overinvolved in specifics, he read and personally signed papers that other presidents left for clerks. He had learned the importance of minutiae in the nation's foreign service, but as chief executive, he was soon complaining that he did not even have time to say his prayers, though he was not a religious man.

Because his administration followed that of his fellow Democrat Pierce, Buchanan astutely left in place efficient loyal party men until their designated terms ended—his version of a modified rotation policy. By reserving some positions, he would use these as a lever for support and fundraising in the later years of his term. His intention, of course, was to shape a reliable, popular coalition of national Democrats loyal to him and thereby defeat the Republicans and humiliate Douglas's supporters. With these dangerous partisans defeated, the sectional controversies would cease, or at least so Buchanan expected.

But the president did not consistently apply, nor make explicit, this policy. Soon a disproportionate number of northerners were removed, some without cause. (One outstanding exception was a U.S. district attorney in Massachusetts who had enforced the return to Virginia from Boston of the fugitive slave Anthony Burns in 1854 and for this action was a hero in the South.) Meanwhile most southerners retained their positions so as not to aggravate their sponsors. Especially northerners with ties to Pierce and Douglas found themselves replaced, as the victorious Buchanan Democrats followed Marcy's injunction that to the victor belongs the spoils. But by such a policy, the president alienated Democrats in the North.

With what some contemporaries described as an old bachelor's fussiness, he berated Congress for its tardy approval of legislation at the end of each session, which left no time for chief executives to give proper attention to legislation they must sign. Nor was he diplomatic in his treatment of his vice president, John Breckinridge, who arrived one day at the

White House soon after the inauguration for a private interview with the president. Buchanan sent word that the vice president should instead drop in at night and visit Harriet Lane. At the time the vice presidency carried no official or even ceremonial duties, save presiding over the Senate and the possibility of replacing a dead president. It was four years of rest and a good salary, according to some. But Breckinridge was a proud Kentuckian, and he never forgave Buchanan for a slight that recognized the vice president's early support for Pierce and Douglas, the president's antagonists in the 1856 nominating convention.

In a practice that continued for two years, President Buchanan met with his cabinet every afternoon, except Sundays, for several hours. Some observers considered the cabinet a directory with Buchanan their puppet, and indeed Secretary of the Treasury Cobb once joked that Buchanan had disagreed "with the administration." But the better evidence, from Attorney General Jeremiah Black and others, indicates that Buchanan dominated, at least until late 1860, a group that spent its afternoons listening to him and who behind his back referred to him somewhat fearfully as "the Squire." Sometimes the president bullied and chastised the inefficient and the corrupt among them, especially John Floyd, his secretary of war, and Cobb at Treasury. Often he invited his cabinet to dinner, for he considered them part of his family. Probably no cabinet in American history spent as much time with the president as did Buchanan's.

The social life of the White House Buchanan left to his niece Harriet Lane and his twenty-seven-year-old secretary and nephew James Buchanan Henry. The resident permanent elite of Washington, who watched administrations come and go, had hoped for more festive times after the limited offerings of the Pierces—in mourning for their son, who had died shortly before they arrived in Washington. Harriet obliged with receptions and calling hours, during which her uncle shook hands and teased the pretty wives of official Washington. While Congress was in session he hosted more formal affairs, called state dinners; members of Congress, the courts, and the diplomatic corps—as many as forty at a time—sat for elaborate meals, while the inexperienced Harriet Lane and young James Buchanan Henry hoped their seating arrangements did not violate any protocol.

The president had two principal recreations. Each year he took a two-week vacation at Bedford Springs, where he soaked in the thermal waters and drank twenty glasses of water a day, declaring afterward that he felt rested. And while in Washington he went for unattended afternoon "constitutionals." One day Edmund Ruffin, Virginia's premier secessionist, encountered the president on one of these walks along Pennsylvania Avenue and described the scene: "As we first passed, he had one eye shut, as is his frequent habit and with the other he stared at me as if he thought he knew me."[3]

Three overlapping crises in the first three years of Buchanan's administration preceded the final one in 1860 that led to war. They were not sequential but overlapped in timing and intensity. Given the economic mentality of the times, the first was beyond his, or any nineteenth-century president's, reach. It began in the late spring of 1857 when the New York branch of a respected Ohio corporation suspended payment after trying to call in unrecoverable loans. By summer and fall, like falling dominoes, fourteen hundred state banks and five thousand businesses, including railroads and factories, were bankrupt. Land values plummeted; jobs disappeared in one of those periodic corrections of economic excess that afflict the American economy. In cities in the North desperate men and women took to the streets searching for employment and begging for bread, while the South remained relatively recession-proof, protected by its more stable agricultural system. Southerners attributed the panic to the speculations and borrowings of greedy northern capitalists. Buchanan agreed.

No one expected the president to do much about the economy in these years before government intervention became acceptable practice. And indeed Buchanan did nothing about what became known as the Panic of 1857, announcing in his first annual message that the government was "without the power to extend relief." Instead the president urged the limited therapies of a Jacksonian Democrat: more use of specie, the redemption of the public debt in gold rather than paper money, more restrictions on state banks' freedom to issue paper currency, and no new public works projects by a federal government that was broke and might even require a loan itself. In his account of his administration written after he left office, Buchanan gave himself high marks for reducing the debt of the federal government. But as with many American presidents who promise frugality, during his administration expenses grew by over $10 million or about 15 percent of the budget in 1856. Despite his plans for a balanced budget, Buchanan left Lincoln a deficit of over $17 million.

In the spring of 1857 Buchanan faced a second crisis, and he responded forcefully, using all the executive authority at his disposal. For several years the Mormons in the territory of Utah, led by the indomitable Governor Brigham Young, had challenged the authority of the federal officers in what Young considered his domain. Young, who convinced forty thousand members of the Church of the Latter Day Saints that he was God's prophet on earth, intended to interpret God's covenant with the Saints without any interference from officials sent by Washington. Under his leadership a religious revival had begun, and as the community prospered and became more intensely religious, its independence grew. There was little tolerance for the secular authorities sent from Washington or for their laws.

Appointed the territorial governor in 1850, Young and his agents constantly harassed Indian agents, federal judges, and magistrates. In 1855 he masterminded the assassination of a federal surveyor. Not just federal officers but all outsiders were discouraged from even traveling through the territory, much less settling in the Salt Lake City area. In September 1857 a group of emigrants from Arkansas—en route to California—discovered the danger when Young and his militia were responsible for the worst civilian atrocity in U.S. history. One hundred and twenty-five pioneers were murdered in Mountain Meadows, Utah, in an act that until recently was blamed on the Paiute Indians, but in which the Mormon militia participated and which Brigham Young covered up.

Buchanan was further outraged by the personal behavior of Young, who proudly advertised his polygamy as the husband of seventeen wives and the father of fifty-seven children. Marriage and the family were widely considered "domestic institutions" under local jurisdiction, and as such untouchable by the federal government. Indeed that was what southerners considered slavery. But the bachelor Buchanan, always something of a prude, did not regard polygamy as a domestic institution beyond the federal government's purview. Mormons, according to the president, were modern sodomites challenging national authority in the first internal rebellion in American history. As Buchanan pointed out in his official proclamation authorizing military action, no one in the Mormon community could "express an opinion favorable to this government or even propose to obey its laws, without exposing his life and property to peril."[4]

With much to gain by deflecting attention from an emerging crisis over slavery in the territory of Kansas, in April 1857 Buchanan authorized a military expedition which he misnamed a *posse comitatus*. The term traditionally referred to a group of volunteers called out by local civilian officials, especially on the frontier, not a U.S. Army force of regulars "not to be withdrawn until the inhabitants of that territory shall manifest a proper sense of the duty which they owe to this government." In all some twenty-five hundred troops, along with a new governor and other officials who would replace the treasonous Young, traveled to Utah, arriving too late in the fall for any military actions against the Mormons. Instead, with the snowy passes into Salt Lake defended by Young's militia, the U.S. Army camped nearby at Fort Bridger, its supply wagons on one occasion destroyed by Mormons, waiting to do battle with the Utah militia in the spring.

But by the spring Thomas Kane, a Pennsylvania friend of Buchanan's, convinced the president that he could negotiate a peaceful settlement. Sensitive to the grievances of the Mormons, who called him their "Little Friend," Kane, armed with a letter from Buchanan, hastened to Utah and effected a peaceful solution. By the end of the year a new governor had taken office. Brigham Young no longer challenged the secular authority of the United States, although his provocation to its moral sensibilities continued in the form of polygamy. By 1858 the president was taking credit for his successful handling of the Utah crisis. In the West the president had not hesitated to assert the military power of the United States. Two years later some Americans wondered why he did not do so in the South.

Buchanan inherited the third and most crucial of his early presidential crises—that of Kansas. For Americans intent on settling in the West, the territory with its fifty million acres was a prize. For southern Americans, its location between North and South made it essential for the dispersion of slavery throughout the West. Yet for the president, slavery remained an obstacle to the prompt admission of Kansas as a Democratic, possibly slave, but probably free, state. Politically, a Democratic state government in Kansas would offset the preparations for statehood of potentially Republican Minnesota and Oregon. The future control of Congress rested in a battle Americans had been fighting over slavery since the 1820s, with territories the battleground. Buchanan hoped to create a coalition of free-soil and proslave Democrats, with partisan politics trumping in significance any division of opinion over slavery, the latter now constitutionally protected by the Dred Scott decision as private property.

Instead, by 1859 Buchanan had heightened the dangers to the Union with his policies in Kansas. More than any other of his decisions, including those in late 1860, his management of the territory demonstrated not just his commitment to the South, and not just his determination to be a forceful president, but fusing the two, his hardheaded resolve to use the executive power for southern interests. Buchanan turned out to be as stubborn for the South as Andrew Jackson was for the Union, only without Jackson's commanding leadership and loyal supporters.

By the time Buchanan assumed the presidency, there were already two competing territorial governments in an area to be organized under the Kansas-Nebraska Act. Although the act mandated that the people of the territory determine the fate of slavery, the implementation of popular sovereignty had not been easy. Pierce had already fired two governors, and the third resigned the day Buchanan took office. One territorial government with a proslavery legislature and judiciary was located first in Shawnee and later in a small town along the Kaw River called Lecompton. The other was the free state government located in Topeka, fifteen miles to the west.

In the first stages of organizing the territory, prosouthern forces had moved so aggressively and unfairly to take possession of the territory for slavery that a backlash had developed. Many settlers, indifferent to slavery, cared more about their prospects of settling on fertile land; others wanted to ensure that the labor of free white men did not compete with that of slaves on that land. In 1855 proslavery residents had forcefully prevented free-state residents from voting; they had adopted a drastic slave code that limited office holding to proslavery men; they had made any criticism of slavery punishable as a felony; and they had established capital punishment for anyone aiding a fugitive slave. Judicial decisions from Lecompton starkly revealed proslave bias as free-state Kansans rarely received any measure of justice.

To ensure their control, the proslavery community encouraged citizens of Missouri living along the western border of that state to travel across the border into Kansas and vote illegally in elections that hardly represented the will of the majority. The proslave U.S. senator from Missouri, David Atchison, led armed invaders into Kansas, some of whom carried banners heralding "Southern Rights" and "Kansas for the South." Meanwhile election officials turned away free-soil residents who refused to take oaths supporting slavery in Kansas.

Under conditions in which less than a quarter of the electorate voted and sometimes only 10 percent did so, the Lecompton government had nevertheless established an election calendar that would lead to the writing of a state constitution—first the election of convention delegates, then the convening of a constitutional convention that would write the state's first charter, which had to be voted on by citizens and accepted by the U.S. Congress. It was a laborious process, but one that had been followed mostly without incident by every territory on its way to statehood.

Outraged free-soilers had responded by establishing their own government in Topeka. In turn the Topeka government drew up its own code of laws, barring slavery from the territory, along with the settlement of free blacks. Free-soilers encouraged northerners to come to what they intended would be land reserved for white families. Advertisements in northern papers featuring news about organized migrations brought some settlers to the territory and infuriated southerners, who were engaged in their own promotions. The growing majority of settlers opposed slavery in Kansas and were insulted by the aggressive slaveocracy intent on trampling the rights of free white men. They boycotted the Lecompton elections for those of their own Topeka government.

Nothing better illustrates the volatile situation in Kansas than the violence, which was marked by the burning of the free state stronghold of Lawrence by a proslavery militia, the abolitionist John Brown's brutal murder of proslavery settlers along Pottawatomie Creek in the spring of 1856, and the reprisal assassination of Brown's son by proslavery forces. Territorial Kansas supported so much organized violence that a series of incidents was dubbed, with only a little exaggeration, "the Wakarusa War." Although some killing involved frontier arguments over land claims, slavery became the true flash point for hostility. By the time Buchanan took office, a contingent of fifteen hundred U.S. Army troops was trying to keep the peace.

Presidents shared constitutional authority with Congress over the territories, but their power to appoint and instruct governors often determined the course of events. Clearly Buchanan needed to restart the process. Instead the president continued to support the Lecompton government, arguing that it was the officially recognized territorial structure. A more evenhanded approach might have begun with a new census, a new registration, and the relocation of the capital in another town. Yet Lecompton, entirely controlled by proslavery Kansans, remained the capital recognized by Washington throughout Buchanan's administration. Hardly conducive to the expression of democracy, the town boasted a large wooden shack as its only public facility, one muddy street, and too many taverns where corrupt federal office holders drank and gambled with the proslavery militia.

Buchanan did appoint a promising new territorial governor. Robert Walker had been born in Pennsylvania and had moved to Mississippi as a young man. Buchanan had known and respected Walker from their shared time in the Senate in the 1830s and in Polk's cabinet during the 1840s where Walker served as secretary of the Treasury. But Kansas was the graveyard of governors, and an irritated president had to make a personal plea to Walker's wife, who thought the position not only dangerous but underpaid and certainly unworthy of her husband's talents. Buchanan promised Walker—and it was a crucial commitment—that any Kansas constitution must be submitted to the people to approve. Again this was customary procedure, although a few southern states had not done so. Just as the formative document of the United States, the Constitution, had been approved by the people, so nineteenth-century Americans expected that state constitutions would be ratified by a majority of citizens. Buchanan had promised as much.

As Walker left for Kansas in the spring of 1857, Buchanan instructed him that all "bona fide citizens" must vote in such a ratification process. Buchanan repeated his instructions in his annual message to Congress in December 1857: "A constitution shall be submitted to the people of the Territory, [and] they must be protected in their right of voting for or against that instrument and the fair expression of the popular will must not be interrupted by fraud and violence . . . it [is] far from my intention to interfere with the decision of the people of Kansas, either for or against slavery." Yet by 1857 the Topeka government represented three times as many Kansans as did that in Lecompton. Only by fraud could the protection of slavery in the constitution survive the political process.

In the summer of 1857—his first as president—Buchanan paid close attention to political conventions in Georgia and Mississippi, which were threatening secession if Kansas was not accepted as a slave state. As one Georgian wrote Senator Alexander Stephens, the future vice president of the Confederacy, "If Kansas comes in as a free state, Buchanan will richly deserve death and I hope some patriotic man will inflict it."[5] Meanwhile Walker, like two previous governors, had decided that Kansas was destined to become a free state, and the governor had described an "isothermal" line above which, for reasons of climate, slavery was impractical and uneconomic. That line ran through southern Kansas. Secretly, for this was a doctrine offensive to southerners, Buchanan had always believed that slavery would simply expire in environmentally hostile areas in the West. A problem that would solve itself, it did not merit the disturbance of the Union. "Sufficient unto the day is the evil thereof." But in the face of southern pressure, the president now supported the best chance slave supporters had, and that was the Lecompton constitution.

In response to the complaints in August 1857 that federal troops in Kansas had been used against free state residents in Topeka and Lawrence "to force the people of Kansas to obey laws not their own," Buchanan produced a message intended for the South as well as the North. The Dred Scott decision, he said, was now the controlling fact of territorial life. Isothermal lines were irrelevant. Territorial slavery existed in Kansas and in every territory, wherever slaveholders wanted to take their property; "the highest tribunal known to our laws has so decided." An exasperated president wondered how anyone could doubt that slavery could exist in territorial Kansas. Just as the slavery crisis was caused, in Buchanan's view, by abolitionists, so in Kansas the offense lay with supporters of the free Topeka government, who refused to vote in Lecompton-organized elections.

Using a flawed historical comparison, the president professed to be following the "wise example" of Madison, who had not attacked the antiwar Hartford convention during the War of 1812. He would not send the army against Topeka, Buchanan said, "unless they shall attempt to perform some act which will bring them into actual collision with the Constitution and the laws." One Georgian hailed Buchanan's widely reprinted letter as "the greatest State Paper for the South that has ever emanated from the executive chair since the days of Washington." But as it turned out, it was overreaching by the Lecompton government that lost the state to slavery—with Buchanan's help.[6]

In the October 1857 elections organized by the Lecompton government for the territorial legislature and a delegate to the U.S. Congress, voting fraud was so extensive and so obvious that Governor Walker threw out the returns from several counties. Most illegal votes came from along the Missouri border south of Kansas City, Missouri, near Westport and Platte City. Precincts with a dozen homes voted twelve hundred ballots for proslavery candidates; names copied from the Cincinnati directory comprised many of the registration lists. In negating these votes, Walker inflamed southern sentiment and embarrassed Buchanan, who withdrew his support from the governor.

Later in October, the previously elected Lecompton delegates met to frame a constitution. An uninspiring lot, they guaranteed that the right of private property, including slaves, overrode any constitutional or legislative sanctions. Articles in the charter of government also legalized the future of the two hundred slaves already in the state and established a slave code, for the treatment of slaves, based on that of Missouri. Defiant to the end, the sixty, often inebriated delegates decided that their only chance to protect slavery was not to permit a referendum. As authors of the constitution, they would simply approve the document necessary for Kansas statehood and send it to Buchanan, who would submit it to Congress.

But such a process was too blatant, even for Buchanan, who had promised submission of the constitution to Kansans for approval. Federal agents from the Interior Department were dispatched to discuss a compromise. Under pressure from Washington, the convention reluctantly agreed that Kansans would simply vote on slavery, leaving the body of the constitution in place. But existing articles legalized the status of those two hundred slaves already in the state. Such a vote would offer no choice. Kansans, if they could even cast ballots in a fair election, could vote for or against slavery, but not for or against the constitution. This arrangement reminded one free-soil Kansan of tests for guilt in which the accused was thrown into water: if he floated, he was taken out and hanged; if he drowned, he was considered not guilty.

Buchanan had influenced this supposed compromise, thereby violating his pledge to Walker that he would "stand or fall on submission." No one could make a case that the choice given Kansans was legitimate, although Buchanan tried. Walker proclaimed it a fraud and travesty, and as a result became the third failed Kansas governor. Buchanan insisted in his annual message to Congress that under the Kansas-Nebraska Act and the doctrine of popular sovereignty, voters could only vote on the future of slavery. Accordingly, on December 21, 1857, Lecompton Kansans cast ballots for the constitution with slavery or for the constitution without slavery, there being no vote for or against the constitution as a whole. In all 6,143 votes were tallied for the option "with" (over 2,000 of these were fraudulent) and 569 "without." But the vote begged the point, because the much larger disenfranchised free state Topeka community, worried about violence and fraud, boycotted the election. When they did vote under an election organized by their political community three weeks later, in January 1858, 10,266 votes were registered against the Lecompton constitution; only 162 for.

The critical moment of Buchanan's presidency had arrived. Would he accept the Lecompton constitution with its articles protecting current slavery and its establishment of a slave code? Would he lobby for congressional approval of the enabling act that would make Kansas a state and supposedly bring peace and quiet, even if it blatantly violated the popular will? Or would he restart the process as Walker and two former governors of Kansas were urging?

In December 1857 Senator Stephen Douglas, who would face a reelection campaign against Abraham Lincoln in eleven months, met with Buchanan in the White House. Douglas was chairman of the powerful Committee on Territories, which would oversee the passage of any legislation moving Kansas from territory to state. The president had ignored the senator throughout the year. Now, in an interview that Douglas sought, Buchanan handed down his final judgment: he would support the Lecompton constitution. In fact, as he informed Douglas, he had already telegraphed his decision to the acting governor. Advocacy of the Lecompton constitution had become an administration measure, the kind of legislative litmus test that defined party loyalty and must be supported by all Democratic senators, congressmen, local officials, and patronage holders. Douglas bristled, alert to the growing sentiment against slavery in the territories in his home state of Illinois and throughout the Northwest as well as to the palpable violation of the Kansas-Nebraska Act, which he had authored. Buchanan reminded Douglas of the fate of disloyal senators who, after disobeying President Jackson, had found themselves in political purgatory. Since Jackson's day, as Buchanan recalled, no senator had voted against an administration measure and survived. An angry Douglas responded in a retort that in different forms and with different subjects has resonated throughout American history, "Mr. President, Andrew Jackson is dead."[7]

On February 2, 1858, Buchanan transmitted the Lecompton constitution to Congress with an accompanying message. His argument was an attack on Topeka residents, whom he compared to those in rebellion in Utah. Like the Mormons, "with treasonable pertinacity," free state Kansans had defied the legitimate institutions of authority, and these "mercenaries of abolitionism" had created a "revolutionary government" that would spread anarchy throughout the territory. In fact the controversy in Kansas had little to do with freeing slaves and much more to do with making slavery national, but Buchanan had long ago conflated free-soilers, antislavery supporters, and abolitionists into the enemy. And to those who complained about the farcical Lecompton process, Buchanan insisted, incorrectly, that he had never promised to submit the entire constitution, only that portion dealing with the future of slavery. Besides, once peacefully accepted into the Union, Kansans could simply change any provisions about slavery that the majority disapproved. Here again he deceived, for the Lecompton constitution could not be changed for seven years and then only by a laborious amendment process that was easy enough for the Lecompton minority to impede.

To delighted southerners, who had watched an unlikely slave state transformed into a probable one, Buchanan offered his splendid gift in a special message to Congress in February 1858: "Kansas is therefore at this moment as much a slave state as Georgia and South Carolina. Without this the equality of the sovereign states composing the Union would be violated, and the use and enjoyment of a territory acquired by the common treasure of all the States would be closed against the people and property of nearly one-half the members of the confederacy." This last was another of Buchanan's convenient delusions. In fact the white South represented less than 20 percent of the population of the United States.[8]

By 1858 Buchanan had already done a great deal for the South, and now he prepared to do even more by using the full powers of the executive to push the Lecompton constitution through Congress, "naked," in the terminology of the day, without changes, modifications, and criticism. By his calculations the Senate presented no difficulty, with its Democratic majority, two-thirds of whom were from slaveholding states. He was proved right when the Senate voted by a comfortable margin to approve the Lecompton constitution in March.

But the House of Representatives, based on population and therefore always a threat to the South, remained uncertain. There the combined opposition of 106 Know-Nothings and Republicans did not outnumber the 128 Democrats, but there were only 75 Democratic congressmen from slaveholding states. The rest were northerners who lived among constituencies alarmed by aggressive slave supporters in the South and increasingly attracted to the Republicans.

Buchanan promptly went to work. Throughout the spring of 1858, using tactics often assumed to be the creation of twentieth-century chief executives, the president sent cabinet members to lobby congressmen. Contracts for shipbuilding and mail routes were dangled before wavering representatives; commissions, patronage jobs (either removals or extensions), funds for newspapers that favored Lecompton, and even cash were offered. Two years later a House committee investigating whether the president had "by money, patronage or other improper means sought to influence the action of Congress" on its Lecompton votes darkly suggested that even prostitutes were offered to recalcitrant legislators. There was no paper trail to the president himself, but by the spring of 1858 most of official Washington agreed that the power of the executive had bought congressmen "like hogs." Meanwhile the administration's newspaper, the *Washington Union*, turned itself into an advertisement for the merits of the Lecompton constitution. Some of its editorials, probably written by Attorney General Black and possibly by the president himself, suggested that slavery was moving north. Kansas was only the beginning.

Despite the pressure of the administration, Buchanan lost the vote in the House, in part because his own Democrats—those from the North led by Stephen Douglas—saw Lecompton as a swindle and voted against it. Earlier Douglas, referring to his support of the president in the 1856 convention, had sworn that as he had "made" Buchanan president, so he would now unmake him. The president, refusing to compromise, shortly provided Douglas with an opportunity.

Here was another turning point in the Buchanan presidency. Buchanan could have sent the constitution back to Kansas and encouraged the writing of a new charter with both groups represented in a new convention. Instead, under his direction new legislation, called the English bill, offered Kansans a bribe. This bribe was not of land, as has been frequently charged, but rather of timing. Kansans had only to vote for the Lecompton constitution and receive the traditional land grant of four million federal acres for the state to enter the Union immediately. But if Kansans rejected Lecompton, they would be penalized and would have to wait until their population reached ninety-three thousand—the number of residents on which representation in the House was based during the 1850s. Barely, with the ranks of the northern Democrats breached, the English bill passed. But Kansans had the last word.

That August when they voted on the Lecompton constitution, 11,300 Kansans voted against the slave document that the president had tried to foist upon them. Fewer than 1,800 residents voted in favor of Lecompton in a fair election; not one of the territory's twenty-eight counties gave Lecompton a majority. The people, so long stifled by the Buchanan administration and an aggressive minority of proslavery Kansans, had spoken. Now there was a new vote for delegates to a constitutional convention, and after the antislavery "Wyandotte" constitution was adopted, ratified by the people of Kansas, and sent to Congress, where it was bitterly opposed by southern congressmen and senators, Kansas entered the Union in January 1861.

In his annual message to Congress in December 1858, Buchanan took credit for resolving the Kansas conflict. With the insouciance that often marked his failures, he noted his pleasure that the excitement in Kansas over slavery had been resolved. "Kansas is tranquil and prosperous." True enough, but he drew the wrong lesson from the controversy, again blaming "the revolutionary" government in Topeka and charging it with resisting lawful authority. In a classic Buchananism, he held that voting on the whole constitution had little to do with the lives of most Kansans and was "insignificant." As a president who treasured the past and never looked to the future, he was surprised that the entire affair had kindled so much controversy. In this long public message, Buchanan devoted disproportionate attention to the foreign policy issues to which, now that his three crises of the economy, Utah, and Kansas were over, he might turn.

He was too optimistic. Slavery was the central issue of his times and had been for over a generation. By taking the side of the South, Buchanan had split the Democrats, and in the process he had ensured his nightmare: the election of a Republican in 1860. Moreover he turned the Democratic party into a southern organization. In effect his politics were as sectional as those of the Republicans, about whom he complained so endlessly. Buchanan's aggressive prosouthernism angered northerners, who feared a slaveholding oligarchy would soon control their government as had almost happened in Kansas. In his famous debates with Stephen Douglas in the fall of 1858, Lincoln held "James" (Buchanan) to be a coconspirator along with "Roger" (Taney), "Franklin" (Pierce), and of course his senatorial opponent, "Stephen" (Douglas), in their efforts to protect slavery everywhere in the United States.

The destructive effects of the president's policy were immediately apparent in the 1858 fall congressional elections when a disproportionate number of northern Democrats lost, especially the doughfaces loyal to the administration. Nowhere was the reaction against Buchanan more obvious than in his home state of Pennsylvania, where the Democratic vote fell by 20 percent. Even the president's friend Glancy Jones was defeated for Congress by what Buchanan denigrated as "conspirators and hounds." To Harriet, in a letter written in the fall of 1858, he admitted, "We have met the enemy . . . and we are theirs." But with two years left in his presidential term, a still confident James Buchanan showed no signs of moderating his aggressive southern stands.

4

Appeasing the South:
The Final Months of the
Buchanan Presidency

The last year of Buchanan's presidency was the worst time in his life. He had hoped after "solving" the crises of his administration in Utah and Kansas that he could turn to his specialty of foreign affairs. In matters of diplomacy, while the American chief executive certainly did not have unlimited power, at least under the Constitution Buchanan interpreted so narrowly, he had more authority than was the case in domestic affairs. Serving as his own secretary of state—for the septuagenarian holder of that title, Lewis Cass, was inattentive—the president intended to check British imperialism in Central America and to rewrite the Clayton-Bulwer Treaty. The latter he considered a colossal diplomatic mistake that limited America's unilateral control over any future canal connecting the Atlantic and Pacific. He hoped as well to get the British out of the Western Hemisphere (with Canada a notable exception), or at least to minimize their presence.

Buchanan's foreign initiatives favored the South, just as his domestic policy did. It seemed obvious to him that the expansion of the United States would proceed southward into Mexico and Central America. Other supporters of manifest destiny had given up the raw American aspirations of the 1840s, but Buchanan stubbornly persisted until the British eventually began the process of ceding the Bay Islands to Honduras and giving sovereignty over the indigenous Mosquito Indians to Nicaragua. The president meant as well to buy Cuba, the island that for nearly thirty years had been his obsession. He continued to argue, as he had in the Ostend Manifesto, that the "Pearl of the Antilles" was essential to American security. And of course he knew that his southern friends eyed it as the Republic's sixteenth slave state with its four hundred thousand slaves.

Hardly timid and vacillating, as he is sometimes considered, Buchanan went further in his imperial ambitions. He sought an American protectorate over parts of northwest Mexico in Chihuahua and Sonora where he described "hostile and Predatory Indians roam[ing] promiscuously." Ahead of his time—for twentieth-century presidents relied on similar explanations for their incursions into Latin America—Buchanan pointed to the mistreatment of Americans as well as the security of their investments during a period of civil war in Mexico.

In his 1858 and 1859 messages to Congress, the president displayed his desire to shift the focus to foreign policy. In fact nearly half his comments in both these years centered on the relations of the United States with places formerly as remote as Japan, China, and Alaska. His proposal for Mexico was the most dramatic. He asked for authority to establish military posts across the Arizona border in Mexican territory, and he requested, from a skeptical Congress, the raising of a military force to enter Mexico, according to his 1859 message, "for the purpose of obtaining indemnity for the past and security for the future . . . I purposely refrain from any suggestion as to whether this force shall consist of regular troops or volunteers or both."

Of course Buchanan was too experienced in public affairs not to anticipate objections to any such action. Republicans and many northern Democrats considered the invasion of Mexico gross interference in the domestic affairs of another nation. Besides it was illegal to use American troops to invade another nation without a declaration of war by Congress. But the president held Mexico an exception to such constitutional strictures. It was a neighbor whose "anarchy and confusion" affected Americans. "As a good neighbor shall we not extend to her a helping hand to save her?"

Republicans, who held over 40 percent of the seats in the thirty-fifth House of Representatives and who found allies among a contingent of third-party representatives, were shocked. In the end Congress either avoided or opposed most of Buchanan's agenda. No legislation ever reached the floor of either house for a vote on his Mexican or Cuban proposals. Even a few southerners and representatives from slave border states who had the most to gain feared the transformation of the federal government into an imperial state whose newly discovered powers might be used against them.

Even in his final annual message to Congress in December 1860, as the cotton states of the South prepared to secede, a stubborn president asked that body to appropriate $30 million for the purchase of Cuba, although it had never been clear that Spain was willing to sell the island. And in this same message, Buchanan repeated his call for funds for an expeditionary force to be sent into Mexico. But Congress continued to be deaf to the chief executive's plans. Buchanan, a lame duck in a political climate favoring the Republicans, had used up his goodwill in the brutal legislative fight over the Lecompton constitution. And after the 1860 elections, Republicans controlled both Congress and the executive.

Measured against other presidents, even those in the twentieth and twenty-first centuries, Buchanan is one of the most aggressive, hawkish chief executives in American history. Few slights from other nations or possible rationales for engagement overseas went unnoticed by this prickly chief executive. Buchanan aspired to be a decisive, aggressive president, even if his international agenda failed. Mostly Buchanan gained approval from southerners, many of whom supported filibustering operations into Central America that violated neutrality laws. Buchanan did not go this far.

The most persistent of these freebooters, William Walker, slipped by patrols, established himself as the unelected leader of Nicaragua, and was captured by Commodore Hiram Paulding and returned by the U.S. Navy to New Orleans. While Buchanan intended to follow the neutrality laws that made Walker's activities illegal, the president considered the filibusterer's arrest to be illegal because it had taken place on foreign soil in Nicaragua. Therefore Commodore Paulding had exceeded his instructions. So Paulding was reprimanded; Walker was released, only to return again to the Central American nation, where he was eventually killed. In this episode Buchanan again played to his southern audience.

In other international maneuvers, the president unhesitatingly sent U.S. troops to the Northwest when Americans and the British became entangled in a dispute over the boundary through the Strait of Juan de Fuca. Off to the Puget Sound went troops under no less than the commander of the army, General Winfield Scott. Eventually a peaceful settlement was negotiated. At the same time the president was asserting American power in another testy disagreement with the British, who were engaged in the practice of stopping and searching possible slave-trading vessels flying the American flag in the Caribbean. Buchanan vigorously opposed the slave trade, but despite an international treaty, the Americans were notoriously lax about ending it, compared to the British. Knowing this, slavers of every country ran up the American flag for protection from the British, and Her Majesty's fleet sometimes stopped and searched them. Buchanan, remembering the reasons his nation had fought the War of 1812, protested such dishonor to the flag. The English had no right to stop any ship sailing under the Stars and Stripes, and eventually, after several strong pronouncements on the subject and the mobilization of the U.S. Navy, the British ordered their West Indies fleet home.

To those who complained that the war-making power belonged only to Congress, Buchanan anticipated modern presidents with his explanation that Congress often could act only "after the mischief has been done." Buchanan wanted a preemptive authorization from Congress so that he could respond immediately to any challenge that he, as the chief executive in charge of foreign affairs, detected. He did not go quite as far as some twentieth-century presidents in asserting his power to use military force overseas, but he was only a step behind.

In perhaps the most ludicrous assertion of American power during his administration, Buchanan ordered twenty-five hundred sailors and marines along with nineteen warships with two hundred guns to punish landlocked Paraguay. That nation's transgression had been to appropriate property claimed by Americans living in Paraguay, to fire on an American ship surveying in the country, and to kill its captain. It took months for this force, approved by Congress in a costly expedition, to move up the Paraná and Paraguay rivers into Asunción, and of course it took months more to come home in 1859. In the meantime these men and ships could have been employed in reinforcing American coastal forts, where they were needed to prevent attacks by seceding southern states, rather than fending off distant insults to the flag. Instead secession was only encouraged by the feeble response of the U.S. government.

In his final year as president Buchanan suffered further humiliations. For years he had unfairly stigmatized the Republicans as a party of treason—an organization whose positions on slavery he believed encouraged bloodthirsty zealots like John Brown and in turn made southern matrons terrified of potential slave uprisings. The president had always considered the Republicans to be not much more than a group of abolitionist preachers and fanatics. He hated New England (the only section of the United States he never visited) and decried its "isms." Once he complained, no doubt with his proper, nonpolitical first lady as his model, that antislavery societies in New England fostered "haranguing" women and that Boston was a terrible place to live.

Partly because of Buchanan's intransigence in Kansas, the Republicans became the nation's majority party after the 1858 congressional elections. In Buchanan's last two years as president Republicans controlled the Thirty-sixth Congress with 114 seats, an increase of 22 seats in two years. Meanwhile his own Democrats, who had dominated the House in the early 1850s, lost 28 seats, though none in the Senate. But the

Republicans still gained 5 seats there. Now in control of the House, Republican party leaders responded to Buchanan's vitriolic antagonism by establishing a special committee investigating corruption in his administration.

Republicans chose "Honest John" Covode, a respected Pennsylvania congressman, to chair this examination into whether Buchanan or any of his administration "by money, patronage or other improper means" had tried to influence Congress. The focus was on the practices used by the president and his cabinet to pass the Lecompton constitution, but soon a wider net was cast. The administration's use of patronage came under investigation, as did payroll taxes levied on patronage holders at election time, changes in post office personnel, bribing voters, and especially granting lucrative government printing contracts to supporters, who then returned a portion of their profits to the party. Of course many were accepted electoral features employed by all parties, but Buchanan's extravagant use of them seemed even to some Democrats to cross the line from permissible practices to indictable offenses. If the president could be tied to them, impeachment was possible. Politicians and civil servants who had long observed the abuses of American politics believed that Buchanan's Buchaneers—the inner circle of friends and members of his administration—had reached unacceptable levels in terms of the use of public authority and funds for private and party profit.

Buchanan dismissed the entire House investigation as an inquisition, calling the witnesses who appeared for five months in the spring of 1860 before the Covode Committee disappointed patronage seekers, informers, and parasites trying to curry favor. But they included several of his influential allies and friends, whose testimony further diminished his credibility. Made up of three Republicans and one Democrat, the committee was undeniably partisan, and it afforded the president no opportunity to respond. Testimony taken in secret and information damaging to the president were leaked into the gossipy salons of Washington. Despite the unfairness, there was considerable evidence that the president's reckless efforts to bulldoze the Lecompton constitution through Congress in the spring of 1858 had involved several forms of bribery, through third parties, of congressmen.

In 1858 relatives of Democrats in the House had received army contracts. Patronage holders had been ordered to vote for the administration bill on Lecompton or their relatives would be removed from office. Cash changed hands. Buchanan also had used appointive positions to punish Stephen Douglas. He had replaced the senator's men with his own and, in clear violation of party unity, had run his pro-Lecompton followers against Douglas's in an unsuccessful effort to take over the Democratic party in Illinois. There was testimony that the administration had used public funds to strengthen his faction of the Democratic organization.[1]

Buchanan pronounced himself above personal corruption. No doubt he was, for he was too rich to take money for himself. But he was never above employing public money in order to further the purposes of his administration and his place in history. His self-described frugality in government was compromised by lavish printing and binding contracts handed out during his years as president.

Certainly his cabinet officers were among the most corrupt in American history. Secretary of the Interior Jacob Thompson sent agents to Kansas to further the administration's interests, paying for them out of his department's funds. Secretary of War John Floyd undersold Fort Snelling, an army post in Minnesota, to a consortium that included a fellow Virginia Democrat and friend. In other instances the War Department bought worthless carbines from favored companies, agreed to pay inflated prices for desired real estate necessary for its installations, and overpaid Democratic contractors. One stalwart army officer, Montgomery Meigs, in charge of projects around Washington, became so outspoken about graft and inefficiency that his protests resulted in his exile to the miserable Florida islands of Dry Tortugas. The Navy Department, again through agents, bought prohibitively expensive coal from a politically well-connected company that give kickbacks to the national Democratic party. The scandals even reached into the president's family when evidence surfaced that Buchanan's nephew by marriage and the brother of the Philadelphia collector of the port, whose name never appeared on the official list of port employees, still turned up at the port—but only on paydays for work never observed by anyone else.

In the course of the investigation Buchanan sent two messages to the House denying on constitutional grounds that Congress had any authority over the executive branch of government. The only exception, said the president, occurred during impeachment hearings before the Judiciary Committee, but the Covode Committee was only an investigating committee on its way to a censure resolution. The president argued as well that, in the event of an impeachment, his accusers would become his judges. In his lofty constitutional style Buchanan noted that the executive and legislative branches were coordinate and had no authority to investigate each other. "I defy all investigations. Nothing but perjury can sully my name." The committee responded that there had been three earlier congressional investigations of corruption in the executive branch that had not risen to the level of impeachment, as indeed the Covode Committee's findings did not. Buchanan exulted in the fact that no criminal charges were preferred, but many citizens were shocked at the amount of graft permeating all agencies and levels of the Buchanan government.

For any assessment of the Buchanan administration, the question remains why this particular president—so experienced in the ways of Washington and so insistent on probity—could have presided over such abuses. The most eloquent portion of Buchanan's inaugural address in March 1857 had referred to the "duty of preserving the government free from the taint or even the suspicion of corruption. Public virtue is the vital spirit of republics and history shows that when this has decayed and the love of money has usurped its place, although the forms of free government may remain for a season, the substance has departed forever."

There were two principal reasons why Buchanan encouraged, or at the very least tolerated, corruption during the Lecompton crisis and did not police his subordinates, thereby destroying his own reputation. First, his pugnacious activism as a chief executive overrode any restraint during the catastrophic fight over the Lecompton constitution. He believed that he could go home to Wheatland having saved the Union by ending the controversy over slavery in the territories. And that required moving Kansas to statehood. His experience and age delivered him into a cocoon of overconfidence, as the end came to justify any means. Second, as the protector of the South and the benefactor of that section's electoral college largesse, he wished to keep southerners in his cabinet. If he fired Floyd, the ever-irascible South would erupt and accuse him of disloyalty. His best opportunity for keeping the Union intact was to maintain the status quo; his best friends in this project were, ironically, southerners.

But increasingly Buchanan's Union was an untenable proposition. It seemed to most nineteenth-century Americans a republic of contradictions—a free nation for whites with slavery for all blacks in the territories and, according to the Dred Scott decision, in the future even in nonslaveholding states. It was as well a democracy dedicated to majority rule controlled by an aggressive sectional minority of southerners. As a consequence of his certitude and his prosouthernism, Buchanan exceeded the normal limits of mid-nineteenth-century partisan behavior. But as was the case with his strong-arm tactics in Kansas, his refusal to deal with the misdeeds of the members of his administration gave the Republicans more ammunition.

During this trying period of his presidency, Buchanan further soured his relations with Congress, from whom he sought appropriations and agreement for his overseas policies, by vetoing several prize pieces of Republican legislation including the Homestead Act. A popular policy in the Northwest, the Homestead Act gave 160 acres of public land free to each settler after five years. Buchanan, on the wrong side of this scintillating expression of American democracy, argued in his veto message that it was not fair to previous settlers to give away free land, that the federal government had no constitutional power to do so, and that the bill was especially unfair to the older states of the Union—a group that included many southern states. Earlier he had vetoed a bill to use public lands to establish land-grant agricultural colleges. Both were measures opposed by southern congressmen and senators, and in both cases, despite congressional approval, Buchanan held that the federal government was exceeding its constitutional authority.

During the presidential election year of 1860 Buchanan paid an obvious price for his intransigence. As voting day approached, Republicans circulated thousands of copies of the Covode Committee's investigation as a campaign document. In the West and Northwest, where the homestead principle was endorsed by some Democrats, Buchanan was excoriated by members of his own party. And to the many Americans who viewed education as an important lever for progress, his veto of legislation to establish land-grant colleges seemed regressive.

The president paid an additional price in credibility when at his party's 1860 nominating convention in Charleston, South Carolina, Democrats divided over their platform concerning slavery in the territories. With the two-thirds rule protecting the South and after several walkouts and reconvenings, the party split. In this dispute the legacy of Buchanan's Kansas policy appeared in the candidacy of two Democrats: Buchanan's enemy Stephen Douglas and John Breckinridge, the southern candidate and Buchanan's vice president whom the president had so nonchalantly overlooked throughout his presidency. Douglas and Breckinridge agreed about nearly everything, including the authority of the Dred Scott decision to protect slavery in the territories. But Breckinridge's faction went further to demand that the federal government protect slavery in the territories—in other words, those who voted for Breckinridge favored a federal slave code.

Neutrality would have been the more politic stance for the president, given the possibility of a fusion ticket or the withdrawal of one of the candidates or perhaps both, with Buchanan favoring his Georgia-born secretary of the Treasury, Howell Cobb, as a replacement. An effective president would have influenced his party members to redo the failed nomination process. But nobody listened to Buchanan anymore. So he tepidly supported Breckinridge, who received the fund-raising aid of the presidency as well as the in-kind services of numerous clerks in various executive departments. In a speech delivered from the White House portico in the summer of 1860, Buchanan explained to a cheering crowd that he favored the Kentuckian because Breckinridge stood for a federal slave code. Slaves in the United States were private property, and as property the rights of white masters must be protected in the territories. Territorial legislatures had no power to abolish slavery, and when the right of property was violated, the federal government must redress the trespass. Under this doctrine Stephen Douglas's popular sovereignty was dead, killed by both president and Supreme Court.

In the voting that followed in November 1860 the Republican Abraham Lincoln won both the electoral vote and a plurality of the popular vote in a four-way election that featured the two Democrats, along with John Bell of the Constitutional Union party. The election ushered in Republican domination of national politics; Buchanan was the last Democratic president for twenty-four years, until Grover Cleveland was elected in 1884. Lincoln won because his support was concentrated in heavily populated northern states with high electoral counts. But as historians have noted, he would have won the electoral vote without the split in the Democratic party,

although the combined popular vote for Douglas and Breckinridge of 2,225,000 was more than his 1,866,452.

Such a conclusion overlooks the significance of the division
in the Democratic party, which with one candidate—and that
candidate was obviously Stephen Douglas, who even campaigned in the South—would have been more attractive to
voters. Douglas had appealed to Unionists in the South, campaigning vigorously against secessionists, who seemed to have
the upper hand only in South Carolina. Not only would
Democratic resources have been more efficiently mobilized
behind one man, but states that voted for Bell like Tennessee
and Virginia might well have supported a single Democratic
candidate, who might also have carried states like Indiana and
Ohio. In fact a united Democratic party might have forestalled
Bell's candidacy entirely.

Buchanan had been largely responsible for this split in his
party. He had done nothing after the fury over Lecompton to
try to reunite the Democratic wings. Indeed he had continued
his vendetta against Douglas by opposing any Democrat who
supported the Illinois senator's position on popular sovereignty, and nowhere more vehemently than in his home state
of Pennsylvania. Buchanan disdained any reunion of the factions, calling on all Democrats—not just those in the South—
to support the Dred Scott decision and its doctrine of protection of slavery in the territories. Northern Democrats must
give up popular sovereignty, for "without self-degradation the
Southern States cannot abandon this equality of states." A
southern slogan of the time, "the equality of states" held that
property in slaves must be on the same footing as all other
property, from gold to horses, from pianos to mattresses. For
Buchanan there would be no waffling on the issue of prohibit-

ing territorial legislatures from outlawing slavery at any stage before statehood. Thus the president who cared so much about the Union had done a great deal to destroy one of the instruments for its survival—the Democratic party.[2]

Disruption of the Union was not yet inevitable. Before the election of Lincoln, secession even among the seven states of the lower South that formed the Confederacy in February 1861 depended on a series of events and decisions in which Buchanan's appeasement of the South figured prominently. In fact, after their success in the off-year congressional elections in 1858, Republicans had lost nine seats in the House in 1860, and given the number of third-party legislators, they did not control either house—provided the southerners stayed in Washington. In four years another presidential election might reverse political fortunes and bring a united Democratic party to power, a point that the ultrapartisan Buchanan made in his address to Congress in 1860.

Immediately after Lincoln's election Buchanan faced the last, most devastating, and personally most wrenching crisis of his life. For months the extreme wing of the prosouthern party in the lower South, especially in South Carolina, had warned that the election of Lincoln, whom they exaggerated into an abolitionist, would justify secession. Under a so-called Black Republican, slavery would not be safe. Of course there were latent reasons for this outbreak of secessionism in 1860: a long-brewing independence movement; the internal dynamics of southern politics that challenged control by planters; fierce antagonism toward northerners; the vaunted southern pride and honor waiting to spill over into martial action; and even the hot, dry, aggravating summer that set tempers on edge. Some said that Lincoln's election was only a pretext.

Southerners had threatened secession for years. In South Carolina the crisis had been simmering since the 1830s nullification fight over federal tariff legislation, though threats to leave the Union had never been as explicit or vehement as in 1860. Buchanan's southern friends had warned a skeptical president during the fall that the election of Lincoln would trigger the end of the Union. They also informed him of the growing restiveness of their slaves, knowing that the danger of slave insurrection was of particular concern for him. Buchanan agreed that northern agitation had inspired slaves with "vague notions of freedom" and had undermined "the sense of security around the family altar," and said so in his message to Congress after Lincoln's election. Rebellious southerners also intimated that any challenge to their departure would lead to a bloody civil war, unless Buchanan kept the peace by handing over government property.

As early as October the president heard from his wary General-in-Chief of the Army, Winfield Scott, who advised that several states would secede if Lincoln was elected. Accordingly Scott, amid other less practical ideas, called for the immediate garrisoning of the federal forts in the South with sufficient troops as to prevent a surprise attack. Showing the flag in any way during this uncertain period was good counsel, though it came with the advisory that only five regiments were available. Of course there were units that could quickly be recalled from western outposts, where many of the sixteen thousand army troops were stationed. But Buchanan disliked both Scott and the advice, and so did nothing. Perhaps to expect that he would do anything before secession is unreasonable, although he was responsive and activist in his foreign policy. One wonders if Stephen Douglas had been president whether he would have been so complacent. Certainly Buchanan's inactivity, like much of his performance in the 120 days left in his administration, reflected his consistent prosouthernism. For it was indubitably to the advantage of the future Confederacy first to have as many states as possible secede, and then to have time to organize a government and prepare an army without challenges from the federal government.

South Carolina wasted no time and joyfully seceded on December 20. The state had always been the most radical southern community in the United States. In the 1830s its state legislature had called a federal tariff act null and void. It was the home of John C. Calhoun, who had promoted the idea of a federal slave code as early as the 1830s and who had argued for a concurrent presidency, one chief executive from the North and one from the South, in order to protect the minority rights of a section that was rapidly losing ground in population and states. Because of its archaic electoral procedures—the state's presidential electors were still chosen by the state legislature—the South Carolina assembly remained in session after the presidential election in November, primed not just to cast its votes for Breckinridge but also to call for a secession convention. Delegates to the latter were duly elected, and in turn they passed a secession ordinance, dissolving ties with the United States and taking their place "as a separate and independent state." Like an untreated contagious disease, the movement spread to other states of the lower South, which also began the process of calling secessionist conventions.

Yet in every one of these states there was a significant pro-Union party, whose members counseled patience. Even in South Carolina radicals like Robert Barnwell Rhett faced opposition from those who continued to revere the Union and to recoil from the possibility of civil war. It was to these men, some of whom were in Washington, that Buchanan needed to turn if he would isolate South Carolina, limit the number of seceding states, and, in his personal ambition, keep the peace, at least until Abraham Lincoln became president in March. To accomplish this, he would need moderates among his advisers. They would need to get the patronage positions that the president had shuffled with such brutal haste during the Lecompton struggle. Clearly Buchanan knew how to do this. Since Andrew Jackson no president had so effectively demonstrated the ways in which the patronage could be marshaled to change the minds of public officials.

Buchanan addressed the legality of secession in his annual message to Congress in early December. Disappointing southern members of his cabinet as well as his friends throughout the South who had every reason to expect a more acquiescent approach to their disloyalty, Buchanan denied the constitutional right to secede. No government installed an entitlement to its own suicide, argued Buchanan. The United States was not a rope of sand to be broken into fragments "whenever any sudden excitement might impel them to such a course." Of course Abraham Lincoln's election was not a minor incident. For Buchanan it represented the culmination of years of northern agitation against the South, but it was a reversible decision. Revolutionary resistance to the federal government, said Buchanan, required "a deliberate, palpable, and dangerous exercise of powers not granted by the Constitution." Lincoln's election did not rise to this level, although Buchanan was suspicious that his actions as president probably would. Soon angry southern congressmen including Jefferson Davis, the senator from Mississippi and future president of the Confederacy, flooded the White House to argue with the president. His favorite cabinet officer, Howell Cobb, who had often shared Buchanan's White House quarters, resigned in protest of the president's position on secession, well before his home state of Georgia left the Union.

At the same time Buchanan extended an encouraging olive branch to seceding states in his denial of federal authority over their actions. They could go in peace, for neither he nor Congress had the power to declare and make war on them. In the view of this presidential student of the Constitution, the power to coerce a state (even though secession was illegal) could not be found among the enumerated powers granted to Congress or president. "It is," argued Buchanan in his December message, "equally apparent that its exercise is not 'necessary and proper for carrying into execution' any one of these powers." Nor did Congress have such authority.

The same inhibition that had inspired his vetoes of congressional legislation, and the same prosouthern sentiment that had infused his political thinking for years, supported Buchanan's extraordinary contradiction—that he held no coercive power to prevent or overturn an illegal act by a state. In this same message Buchanan disclaimed any power to decide what the government's relation to the seceding states might be. Suddenly a previously forceful executive had withdrawn into a crabbed reading of the Constitution that overlooked those parts of that document that could have been used to sustain federal action. In any case, concluded Buchanan, presidents only executed the laws.

Americans during the secession winter of 1860–61 recalled other presidents who had differently interpreted their oath of office to preserve, protect, and defend the Constitution of the

United States and to execute its laws. During the Whiskey Rebellion of 1794, when Pennsylvanians refused to pay taxes on whiskey, President George Washington, under the authority of the Federal Militia Act and after his proclamation "against combinations subversive of the just authority of the government," had called up the militia and even led it into battle against a group of Pennsylvanians.

Under even the most constrained reading of the militia acts of 1794 and 1807, the president did not have to wait for a request from a federal officer to call up the South Carolina militia in order to execute federal laws such as collecting the revenue, delivering the mail, surveying the public lands, and controlling forts and ordinance facilities. Most northern congressmen believed that the president had the authority, if all federal officers in South Carolina resigned, to appoint new officials in Washington who would ask for help in putting down insurrection. (This was a sticking point because all federal officials in South Carolina resigned, and in a legalism that Buchanan insisted on, no one had asked him—as they must—to intervene.)

If Congress would not confirm his selection of a new federal marshal—for by this time few northern or southern congressmen had any confidence in the president—he could make an emergency appointment and follow the path of his successor, who justified violating one law in order to support the larger, more significant purpose of preserving the Union. And if the power of secessionist public opinion was so strong as to prevent any men from serving in the militia, he could nationalize other militia units. New York had already offered volunteer units he could commission as a *posse comitatus*. Assuredly Buchanan had authority to organize an expeditionary force against a state, as well as against individuals. As he had said in his remarks about the Covode investigation in March 1860, "The people have not confined the presidency to the exercise of executive duties. They have also conferred upon him a large measure of legislative discretion"—discretion he had employed in other episodes during his presidency. Moreover, from another perspective, he could accept South Carolina's definition of itself as a foreign nation, now subject to the same federal authority as Buchanan had imposed on Paraguay.

Northern newspapers recalled Andrew Jackson and his vigorous reaction to South Carolina's ordinance nullifying the 1832 federal tariff and that state's subsequent preparations for war. Jackson had responded forcefully with an immediate presidential proclamation. He had warned South Carolina that states had no right to invalidate any federal law; he had encouraged Congress to pass the Force Bill mobilizing the army; and he had begun readying the navy at Norfolk, along with three units of artillery, to counter South Carolina's actions. Jackson also established communications with Unionists in the state, who worked for an ultimately successful compromise, and he sent his own agents into South Carolina to find ways to protect federal property and even to jail leaders of the nullification movement. He quickly moved collection offices and protected federal agents from assaults by state officials. Simultaneously he prepared the fortifications in Charleston Harbor for attack. Later at least one South Carolinian acknowledged that the president's energy and initiative had chilled the state's taste for nullification and had encouraged compromise.

Though a disciple of Jackson and a model of strong executive power, Buchanan did nothing for two months after Lincoln's election. There was no stern proclamation to South

Carolina, only his annual address to Congress in December. Privately, quoting from the book of Job, the president explained that he intended to come between the factions of the North and South as a daysman (an archaic reference to an arbitrator) "with one hand on the head of each counseling patience." While northern Republican newspapers complained that he brought dishonor to the nation and should be impeached, the New York senator William Henry Seward, soon to be Lincoln's secretary of state, observed that what Buchanan espoused was that no state had a right to secede unless it wanted to and that the government must save the Union unless somebody opposed it.[3]

During December, before six additional states left the Union in January and February, Buchanan's contradiction of illegal state secession cobbled with unlawful federal coercion was enacted into public policy during the struggle over the federal forts, especially those in Charleston Harbor. In the thinking of secessionists state governments owned federal property under the doctrine of eminent domain. Accordingly, throughout the lower South southerners seized forts, customhouses and armories, post offices, and even courtrooms, in some cases before secession and in all cases with no response from the federal government. In Texas southern-sympathizing Major General David Twiggs of the U.S. Army and commander of the Department of Texas, simply surrendered all federal property to the new Confederate government, an action that Buchanan did protest by dismissing the general. But that was in February, not in the early crucial weeks of the crisis. It was in Charleston that the controversy between aggressive secessionists and an appeasing chief executive erupted. For both Buchanan and his successor,

Lincoln, control of Charleston's Fort Sumter became the test of resolve.

In early December General Scott again argued for sending troops and supplies to reinforce the new commander of the federal forces in Charleston, Major Robert Anderson, who was headquartered at Fort Moultrie, one of several federal installations in Charleston Harbor. Located on a peninsula, Fort Moultrie was surrounded by high sand dunes that made it indefensible, unless reinforced, from a land attack that the local militia was increasingly capable of mounting. Across the bay, Fort Sumter, a brick pentagon built on a man-made island three miles from the heart of the city, dominated the harbor. A recent congressional appropriation had underwritten the completion and armament of both installations, and soldiers along with civilian laborers were hard at work.

As the work progressed, South Carolinians raised the ante. Sending commissioners to Washington, they sought a truce of sorts—at least a truce until after their formal secession, when a new government would take over and they would send different agents. If Buchanan promised not to reinforce the forts, they would not attack either. But such a diplomatic maneuver greatly benefited South Carolina and as well the entire secessionist movement throughout the lower South. At the time the state had little artillery and armaments and few soldiers. Local leaders were hurrying to arm and train the militia in Charleston, and while local mobs had already interfered with the efforts of U.S. Army officers to take ammunition from a federal armory, South Carolina needed time. Buchanan gave it to them. Despite his experience as a diplomat, he placed himself in the unfortunate position of implicitly admitting that any reinforcement of the Charleston forts was coercion, even as he maintained the government's defensive right to stay in the forts. In a move that bordered on impropriety, he negotiated with the commissioners as private gentlemen, not authorized emissaries. But any meeting, no matter what their status, gave further encouragement to the South Carolinians. Buchanan should not have had any discussions with men intent on treason. Refusing to promise that he would not reinforce, the president gave every indication that he would do nothing. And he also sent a personal ambassador to Charleston, asking the governor to postpone the state's secession until Lincoln was inaugurated.

Throughout the critical month of December, a nervous president expended time and energy in long sessions with his cabinet. Those around him noticed a new twitch of his cheek as if "spirits were pulling at his jaw." His hair was askew. Usually well informed, he forgot orders that he had given and dispatches that he had read. He gave up his recreational walks around Washington and made his advisers come to the upstairs library, unable some days to lift himself out of bed. He cursed and wept, and his hands trembled. Like Wilson during his campaign for the League of Nations in the summer of 1919 and Nixon in the summer of 1974 before his resignation over Watergate, Buchanan gave every indication of severe mental strain affecting both his health and his judgment.

Buchanan had always been a chief executive who lectured to his advisers, paying limited attention to their ideas, because he was intent on being his own president. But after Cobb's resignation and then that of Cass, who had left because Buchanan had not reinforced the forts, he spent more time listening. When Mississippi chose Secretary of the Interior Jacob Thompson of Mississippi as its agent to discuss secession with North Carolina officials, Buchanan approved Thompson's trip from Washington to Raleigh. The government even paid the secretary's expenses in a mission undertaken to discuss the destruction of that government. Then unexpectedly in late December 1860 an internal emergency overtook his administration.

The president should have long ago gotten rid of Secretary of War Floyd, a known incompetent suspected of fraud. Now it came to light that Floyd had used funds, illegally obtained, in order to pay civilian contractors who did work for the U.S. Army. Floyd had taken negotiable bonds from the Indian trust funds, kept in a wooden chest in the Interior Department, in exchange for drafts from the contracting firm. The firm then sold the bonds and paid its creditors. When funds were received for the army, in a plan that permitted grossly unsupervised accounting, Floyd would repay the money into the Indian funds. But the embezzlement was discovered; a complicit clerk in the Interior Department, who happened to be a cousin of Floyd's wife, was arrested, and the connivance of two secretaries of Buchanan's cabinet was exposed. Buchanan, ever loyal to a cabinet that remained his official and personal family and fearful of disturbing southern opinion, did not fire the Virginian Floyd immediately. Instead he asked the often-reprimanded Floyd for a resignation, which turned out to be slow in coming.

In fact Floyd continued to offer his advice from the sofa he claimed in the president's office during cabinet meetings. In Washington the Virginian was quoted as saying he would cut off his hand before he would order the resupplying and reinforcement of southern coastal forts, which Major Anderson as well as General Scott now sought. Only at the end of December did Floyd resign, deceptively giving as his reason Buchanan's opposition to secession, when in fact it was the result of his fraud. But in another display of his appeasement, Buchanan had not asked for the secretary's resignation because of his obvious disloyalty to the government.

Floyd was responsible for another scandal when it was discovered that he had sent disproportionate numbers of small arms along with ammunition to southern states. In the historical (and later congressional) indictment against Floyd that must include a negligent Buchanan, the Confederates did their fighting with arms sent by one of the more treacherous public officials in American history during one of the nation's most disloyal administrations. Buchanan, in his rationalization of his presidency published in retirement, denied the charge on the grounds that the orders came before southern states contemplated secession, that the firearms were inferior, and that the numbers sent south were not an unreasonable amount. Perhaps, but Floyd, soon to become a Confederate general, undermined the president's case with his later claims in Virginia that he had personally been responsible for sending to southern states many of the arms the Confederate army later used. No one could doubt that Floyd sent significant numbers of the powerful, long-range artillery called Columbiads and thirty-two pounders, along with other heavy ordnance, to two forts in Texas the very day that South Carolina seceded. Only the intervention of a group of angry citizens in Pittsburgh, who informed Buchanan the day before the arms were shipped south, prevented another episode of gross dereliction by a president immobilized by the conflict between his duty to the nation and his preference for the South.

As disunion proceeded and it became clear that seceding states would join in a confederacy, Buchanan continued to surround himself with southerners. He had nothing to do with

Republican leaders. He remained entirely dismissive of their ideas. Throughout November and December, the administration newspaper, the *Washington Constitution,* supported by government printing and widely viewed in Washington as the voice of the president, continued to support secession. Only in January did the president remove his patronage and close down the paper. Not only was his cabinet still dominated by future Confederates (Cass and Black were exceptions who proposed reinforcing the forts), but his informal circle of counselors on which all presidents depend was overwhelmingly from the Deep South. Senator Jefferson Davis, furious over Buchanan's denial of secession on constitutional grounds, continued to advise; so did Robert Toombs of Georgia, Senator John Slidell of Louisiana, and, most dangerously, William Henry Trescot, an assistant secretary of state and a Charleston native, who reported on his conversations with Buchanan to his state government while still a federal officer.

In the informal southern clubs sufficiently organized as to have names like Dixies, Coral Reefers, and Spartans, sensitive information about administrative plans was leaked and sent southward, as federal employees advised southern governors as to how to buy arms from local arsenals and private arms dealers. Even Rose O'Neal Greenhow, the future Confederate spy and a friend of Buchanan's, tried her hand at insider information gathering and trading. And from officials in the seceded states came word to their informants to stay in Washington. No new government ever had so effective an information system about its future enemy.

On Christmas night 1860 Major Anderson moved to Fort Sumter. In a night operation that eluded South Carolinian patrols, sixty soldiers spiked the guns at Fort Moultrie, burned their wooden carriages, and then quietly rowed across the bay from Fort Moultrie to the more defensible Sumter with its fifty-foot walls. There they immediately began the process of strengthening the gun casemates, mounting guns, and closing embrasures. When the news came to Washington, Buchanan despaired: "My God, are calamities never to come singly!" He referred to the growing turmoil within his cabinet and to his special dilemma over the disgraced Floyd.

At the time he was also meeting with a group of postsecession South Carolinian commissioners, and he had let it be known that he would support a truce in Charleston Harbor until Congress, a national convention, or even a special convention—anyone but him—could find a workable compromise acceptable to both sides. Of course Buchanan had his own ideas for appeasing the South. They depended on the passage of constitutional amendments guaranteeing slavery in the states and in the territories and enforcing the right of southerners to reclaim their escaped slaves in the North. In all his plans, the rest of the United States and especially the Republicans must make adjustments to the South's interests.

After Anderson's move to Sumter, a dismayed president faced angry commissioners, who sought the surrender of Fort Sumter, a position that several of his cabinet officers supported. Secretary of the Interior Thompson noted that South Carolina was a small state with a sparse white population. Why not evacuate property that southerners believed they owned under the doctrine of eminent domain? They would buy the fort. Moreover, Anderson had violated the earlier agreements with South Carolina that the state had made with Buchanan—or at least thought that it had made.

But Buchanan could not go this far. Even as his Unionism

clashed with his strong prosouthernism, he knew that he must hold federal property; it was treason to surrender a military post. Nor could the fort, now a symbol of national authority, be quietly taken over, as had happened earlier throughout the coastal South. In his proposed memorandum to the commissioners Buchanan agreed to what he thought would be a peace-keeping compromise, though all his adjustments favored the South: he ordered Anderson back to Fort Moultrie, a death sentence given the ease with which the local militia could invade that installation and, as well, an implicit acknowledgment of the right of secession. In return South Carolina must pledge that it would not molest the forts, and the commissioners must meet with Congress. This latter recommendation gave seditious diplomatic standing to an insurrectionary group. The president also reiterated his earlier noncoercion pledge and, in a further play to the commissioners, agreed with them that Anderson had exceeded his orders. The president was wrong about this last point. When Anderson's orders were produced from the War Department, the commander at Fort Sumter had indeed been authorized to move his force to the most defensible of the Charleston forts, if he had "tangible evidence" of a hostile threat.

By this time the cabinet included three strong Union voices, and Buchanan, less and less in control, depended especially on Attorney General Jeremiah Black, a fellow Pennsylvanian. The departure of southerners had forced Buchanan to choose cabinet officers from the North, whose differences with him revealed just how extreme the president's prosouthern views were. Unable to tolerate the appeasement of South Carolina in the president's draft, Black (appointed secretary of state on December 17), Joseph Holt, and new attorney general

Edwin Stanton argued that to order Anderson back to Moultrie was treason. They would resign if Buchanan did not modify his memorandum. Like several documents and one tape in presidential history, this state paper, conveniently for Buchanan, has disappeared from the record, but, resurrected from other sources, it demonstrated the loyalties of this president. In one account a distraught president asked Black if he too would leave him. Black replied that Buchanan's memorandum "swept the ground from our feet" and placed the president where "no man can stand with you."

Buchanan, in an unusual gesture, asked Black to rewrite the document. The confrontation ended with the president's poignant acknowledgment that he had no friends and could not part with Black, Stanton, and Holt. So the three stayed, and Black's more forceful response denied the right of South Carolina to take over federal property. When the South Carolina commissioners heard this version, they accused Buchanan of not honoring his pledge to them. Rudely, they demanded the evacuation of Sumter. Such arrogance was too much even for Buchanan. The president refused to see them, and they left for a state that was busily mobilizing and planning to seize all the federal facilities in Charleston.[4]

In these crisis-filled days of December the president faced a crossroads and turned onto the pathway of Unionism. Later he would argue that his policies had been consistent throughout. But he deceived himself, for he had been willing to give up Fort Sumter, according to his cabinet officers. Sending Anderson back to the indefensible Moultrie was tantamount to surrendering the national presence in South Carolina. Soon it became impossible because South Carolina had taken over all the federal fortifications in Charleston, including Moultrie.

Keeping the fort was a minimal gesture from the point of view of asserting the power of the federal government. Some historians argue that Buchanan deserves credit for having left Lincoln a hand to play, for without the salvaging of Sumter, the Confederacy could have gone in peace, its principle of lawful secession acknowledged in practice, if not theory. Empowered by the abandonment of any authority over them, certainly the Confederates would have tried to take over the slave border states. As it was, secessionists throughout the South found encouragement in Buchanan's policies—the best president they would ever have, many believed. In assessing the Buchanan presidency, one should note how long it took the president to resist the southerners and even mount a defensive claim on Sumter, how important several cabinet officers were in this decision, and how much Buchanan's delay, grounded in his sectional prejudice, cost the nation. Buchanan was significant in presidential annals for what he did not do and for how slowly he did what he did do. Only if the supposition that the existence of two nations, one holding slaves from shore to shining shore, is justified are Buchanan's policies commendable.

The question remains why Buchanan, a Pennsylvanian educated in a free state whose wealth came from the practices of capitalism, not plantations, was so prosouthern. The answer goes beyond the political support the South extended to him in the election of 1856. Rather, it rests in his social and cultural identification with what he perceived as the southern values of leisure, the gentleman's code of honor, and what George Cary Eggleston, a Virginia writer, once called "a soft dreamy deliciously quiet life . . . with all its sharp corners removed." Throughout his life James Buchanan enjoyed the company of southerners. Their grace and courtesy, even their conversational talents, attracted him. With slavery unimportant—indeed Buchanan became convinced that slavery helped "civilize" blacks—he sought out the company of these white aristocrats and soon absorbed their ideals. He believed that southern legislators were often statesmen, protecting that icon of his faith—the U.S. Constitution. And in his early years in Washington his mentor, Senator William King, had left an indelible impression on him.

The crisis the South had precipitated forced Buchanan to convert to a sterner Unionism. Now the president supported what General Scott and most of his cabinet had been demanding for weeks: he would reinforce Fort Sumter. On January 5, 1861, the *Star of the West*, carrying 250 men and supplies belowdecks, slipped from its anchorage in New York and headed south on the very day that Anderson informed Scott he felt secure and did not need reinforcements. The countermanding order came too late, but a powerful naval vessel, the *Brooklyn*, was ordered to assist if the chartered merchant vessel the *Star of the West* was damaged by battle in Charleston Harbor.

Four days later, warned by their spy network in Washington, the Charleston batteries opened fire on the *Star of the West* as it entered the channel. Several cannonballs skipped across the water, in firing sailors on the Union ship claimed was wild but frightening. Hoping for covering artillery fire from the guns at Sumter, the vessel desperately dipped its flag, a signal of distress. But under orders to keep the peace, the *Star* turned around and moved out to sea without delivering either troops or supplies. Astonishingly, Buchanan had not instructed Major Anderson to respond with covering fire. In fact the president had not informed him of the expedition at all. Lacking any orders, the commander of Fort Sumter did not respond. Later, in a message to South Carolina governor Francis Pickens, Anderson hoped the hostile fire was "without [Pickens's] sanction or authority." Otherwise it was an act of war, but Anderson had no authority to start a war. And in Washington a defiant southern senator, Louis Wigfall of Texas, taunted northerners on the floor of Congress: "[Your] flag ha[s] been insulted; redress it if you dare."[5]

Buchanan had no intention of redressing the humiliation at Sumter, as a period of calm took over. Anderson did not need any reinforcements for the moment, and now the president could turn his attention to supporting the compromise efforts under way in Washington. Another president might have followed up on the January incident, for the flag had been fired on. And in February another plan to reinforce Sumter with warships, proposed by Captain Gustavus Fox, gained the approval of General Scott and others in the administration. Buchanan at first agreed and then withdrew his consent because he considered the truce established after the *Star of the West* incident to be binding. Instead the president sought only to support the feckless compromise efforts of Congress and the Washington Peace Conference, the latter called by the Virginia legislature, which met without any of the seceded states attending.

Finally in March Buchanan's 120 days of agony ended, although he even hesitated about the need for troops in Washington to protect the transfer of power to the new Republican administration. Such a military presence might upset the southerners still in the city, but Scott had no such qualms. The ancient general stationed himself in a carriage on a hill overlooking the Capitol, scanning the horizon for any efforts to disrupt the inauguration. When Buchanan and Lincoln rode to the Capitol, Washington was well defended. On the ride back Buchanan turned to Lincoln and said, "If you are as happy in entering the White House as I shall feel on returning to Wheatland you are a happy man."

Buchanan had a new reason for this sentiment. The night before, a message had come from Major Anderson that he was running out of supplies. Earlier Anderson had warned that he could last for only five months. But given South Carolina's guns and a new floating battery in the harbor, any relief expedition would now require twenty thousand troops and significant naval forces. Instead it was Lincoln who must deal with the problems that Buchanan's inactivity had exacerbated.

Some historians and Buchanan himself insist that Lincoln followed Buchanan's policies insofar as Fort Sumter was concerned. In his inaugural address Lincoln pledged no more than "to hold, occupy, and possess" the forts, and while he declined to go so far as Buchanan to deny the right of coercing the Confederacy, he would not invade. The South would have to attack, which it did six weeks after Lincoln's inauguration when another expedition was nearing the fort.

But the similarities are superficial. Lincoln inherited the effects of Buchanan's appeasement. These had made the Confederacy far more powerful than it might have been. The new president faced an organized government that was as wealthy as many European nations. Buchanan had faced only South Carolina, until the second week of January. Lincoln confronted a Confederacy with a constitution and leaders who were already making their case for diplomatic support in France and Great Britain, and more dangerously in the eight slaveholding states that had not seceded. These states were constrained by the power of southern Unionists and their attachment to the Union. A vigorous reaction to the secession of South Carolina, indeed a strong response to the taking of federal property throughout the cotton states, would have stanched the departure of others. Virginian Edward Pollard used a sailing metaphor to make the point: James Buchanan "drew the wind for southern sails by his complacent attitude." Certainly after the firing on the *Star of the West*, a legitimate casus belli existed, about which Buchanan did nothing. Throughout his presidency Buchanan so exaggerated what the South might do that he was often immobilized, and as Lincoln overestimated the spirit of Unionism in the border states, so Buchanan underestimated it in the South.

It is also worth noting that Lincoln understood the emergency powers of the federal government in a way that Buchanan did not. As the new president wrote in a letter to Erastus Corning in 1863, in cases of rebellion and invasion, he could never be persuaded that the government could not take strong measures not available in peacetime. To illustrate the point, Lincoln used the commonplace analogy of a drug not given to a healthy man, but entirely appropriate to save a sick man.

Americans have conveniently misled themselves about the presidency of James Buchanan, preferring to classify him as indecisive and inactive. According to historian Samuel Eliot Morison, "He prayed, and frittered and did nothing." In fact Buchanan's failing during the crisis over the Union was not inactivity, but rather his partiality for the South, a favoritism that bordered on disloyalty in an officer pledged to defend all the United States. He was that most dangerous of chief executives, a stubborn, mistaken ideologue whose principles held no room for compromise. His experience in government had only rendered him too self-confident to consider other views. In his betrayal of the national trust, Buchanan came closer to committing treason than any other president in American history.

What the president did not do was avoided in the name of prosouthernism, for in other matters his was not a presidency hampered by either feebleness or the lack of understanding of an old public functionary. When he confronted the crisis of Anderson's move to Sumter, he showed his true colors. Only the intervention of his cabinet officers saved the fort. But Buchanan's reputation has been shielded by the need for reconciliation with the South after the Civil War and a version of national history that overemphasizes patriotic visions of chief executives. Better an incompetent than a near traitor.

In his study at Wheatland, where he spent most of his time after the presidency ("age loves home" was one of his sayings), Buchanan worked hard to vindicate his administration. Only Nixon matched his strenuous after-the-fact effort to rehabilitate a failed presidency. Buchanan had hoped that Jeremiah Black, his attorney general and secretary of state, would undertake this project. But Black soon encountered such differences with the former president's version of events, especially those after Lincoln's election, that he withdrew. So the former president worked alone, collecting documents, arguing for the necessity of his policies, and angrily noting the defection of cabinet officers like Stanton, Holt, and Dix who joined the Lincoln administration.

Throughout the war Buchanan was a good Unionist. He supported the draft, but not the Emancipation Proclamation, and he never publicly criticized what he considered Lincoln's violations of the Constitution. Actually the freeing of the slaves gave him an opportunity to join the Presbyterian Church, which he did in 1865. Earlier he had refused to do so, considering that denomination too abolitionist. Buchanan was working on his version of his presidency when the epic battle of Gettysburg took place some twenty miles away, and he wrote a friend that if he were younger, he would take up arms to defend the Union.

In 1866 Buchanan's exculpatory three-hundred-page *Mr. Buchanan's Administration on the Eve of the Rebellion* appeared. The volume was notable for the attention given to northern antislavery agitation and "the malign influence of the Republican party" as the causes of secession and a last chapter that highlighted his foreign policy successes. The world might criticize his performance but, ever stubborn, he was "completely satisfied" with his actions, even those in the frenzied last days of his administration. But the former president found plenty of other culprits—including Major Anderson, who should never have moved to Fort Sumter; General Scott, with whom he carried on an angry newspaper exchange; and especially Congress, which had not heeded any of his warnings or requests for more authority. Two years after his defense was published, his mission complete, James Buchanan died in his bedroom at Wheatland of pneumonia, aged seventy-seven.

Afterword

The question remains why such an experienced and intelligent politician failed so miserably as president of the United States. While all presidencies are idiosyncratic, varying in their contexts and challenges, the issue here is what James Buchanan's mistakes were, why they occurred, and whether they can usefully serve as benchmarks beyond their specific context. Is there something about presidential failures, just as with presidential achievements, that can be teased out to provide a road map, in this case, of ineffectiveness? Somehow the common characteristics and recurrent patterns of successful presidencies are easily classified into categories such as (to use Fred Greenstein's model in *The Presidential Difference* for twentieth-century presidents) ability to communicate, political skill, vision, cognitive style, and emotional intelligence. It is not sufficient to assert that Buchanan was deficient in these categories, because in many ways he was not. Nor should the matter be abandoned to the generalization that all unsuccessful leaders are alike in ways that we cannot categorize, whereas great leaders vary in special ways that deserve to be analyzed.

Certainly there is agreement about Buchanan's failure, although not about its cause. Buchanan makes up the third member of that feckless triumvirate of antebellum presidential losers, along with Millard Fillmore and Franklin Pierce. But more failed even than they, he is usually placed among the very worst of our presidents—an irredeemable group that includes Richard Nixon, Warren Harding, and, in some polls, Ulysses S. Grant. Buchanan's reputation has collapsed even further as Americans have come to appreciate the Civil War's palpable benefits of emancipation and the survival of the Union. Before World War II, when it was fashionable to interpret the Civil War as an avoidable conflict and slavery as a dying institution, historians such as Philip Auchampaugh and George Fort Milton accepted Buchanan's description of his presidency and portrayed him as a peacemaker trying to save the United States from an unnecessary war. It was a prosouthern point of view, nurtured at a time in American history when the South, having lost the war, set about the business of winning it in the history books.

In the period following World War II and the civil rights movement, the portrayal of Buchanan by historians such as Roy Nichols, Kenneth Stampp, and Michael Holt was unremittingly negative. But their historical criticism rested, incorrectly I believe, on the grounds of the president's age, on his long years as a politician, which rendered him unable to rise to the level of a leader during the secession crisis, and on his vacillation in the Sumter crisis. The exception was Elbert Smith's study of the Buchanan presidency, which properly paid attention to the man's central failing as a chief executive—his prosouthernism. But overall, given the importance of his administration, James Buchanan has not attracted much historical interest, mostly because his successor's story is so compelling and his so dismal.

Buchanan's biographers are more sympathetic. Fifteen years after Buchanan died, George Ticknor Curtis, a Democrat who disliked Lincoln, published a two-volume, family-authorized biography that included personal letters and original documents. Convinced that injustice had been done to Buchanan's reputation, Curtis—who shared his subject's rigid interpretation of the U.S. Constitution—followed the former president's own defense. So too did Pennsylvanian Philip Klein in a biography published in 1962. Klein portrayed Buchanan as a peacemaker who confronted events beyond his control. Another loyal Pennsylvanian, the novelist John Updike, wrote a three-act play, *Buchanan Dying*, with bit parts for everyone from Buchanan's housekeeper, Hetty Parker, to Ann Coleman and Charles Sumner. Updike is sympathetic to his hero, who in the moments before his death consoles himself with the thought that "once death has equalized all men, worth flies from their artifacts." But for Buchanan, who is possibly a better subject for novelists than for accusatory historians, the reverse—the disappearance of his flawed reputation—has not occurred.

The explanation of why Buchanan failed so miserably remains a worthwhile historical consideration. How could this avowed nationalist, who said he did not want to outlive the Union, do so much to destroy it? Did he fail because the crisis was beyond the ability of any chief executive to solve and because of his inflexible reading of the Constitution? And what of the structure of the U.S. government that seemingly, at least until new interpretations in the twentieth century, gave Congress so many powers and the executive so few? Did Buchanan fall into the trap of those nineteenth-century presidents who held themselves to be mere administrators? Were Buchanan's failings attributable to the long period between the election of a new president in early November and his inauguration in March, circumstances that made Buchanan into a lame duck during a critical time in American history?

Or was the reason for his miscalculations and poor judgment his personality? Did Buchanan lack the level of emotional intelligence that is clearly observable in some of our best presidents? Did Buchanan have the third-rate temperament that makes it impossible to lead a nation and especially so during a period of crisis? Finally, what exactly were his fatal errors?

Some answers come from a close scrutiny of the three major mistakes of his presidency: his handling of the Kansas crisis, his refusal to act when South Carolina initiated the process of secession in November and December of 1860, and his decision, which was later reversed, to order Major Anderson back to Fort Moultrie. As to the first of these, when Buchanan continued to support the minority proslave Kansas government in Lecompton and its constitution, he did so on the grounds that it was the legal authority in the territory. Arguably he was correct. It was certainly the first one established, but it rested on fraud and violence and was never the legitimate government supported by a majority of citizens in the territory. As president, Buchanan had the authority to restart the process. His power to appoint governors and approve and submit territorial constitutions to Congress could redirect the entire process. But Buchanan did not hear the entreaties of Kansans. Nor did he listen to three of the former territorial governors, nor to most of the northern wing of the Democratic party, all of whom encouraged him to reject

Lecompton. And of course he never listened to the Republicans, whom he despised. Even when he lost the vote in the House of Representatives in early 1858, this president would not give way but instead bludgeoned Congress with another territorial bill, which was eventually repudiated by Kansans in a fair vote that summer.

It is not enough to say that Buchanan was stubborn in the Kansas crisis. Of course he was. But to an experienced official like Buchanan, avoiding a future disaster usually trumps making self-defeating commitments in the present. The real question for his dogged attachment to a failed process is why he would pursue a suicidal course that led to a traumatic division in the Democratic party, thereby ensuring the election of the Republican Abraham Lincoln. In fact Buchanan consistently acknowledged his party as one of the few surviving mechanisms available to keep the nation intact. So why destroy it?

The answer speaks to one of the palpable characteristics of failed presidencies—the arrogant, wrongheaded, uncompromising use of power. Buchanan believed that he could push legislation through Congress that would not only bring Kansas into the Union as a Democratic state but, more important for his own reputation, also solve forever the divisive matter of slavery in the territories. In this instance his experience as a public official worked against him. He assumed—and assumptions are always the heart of arrogance—that he would achieve his goals and would return to Wheatland a national hero.

The structure of the federal government had nothing to do with this failure; a more adroit, flexible politician could have handled the issue by listening to the majority. But, in a second characteristic of most failed presidencies, Buchanan was far too ideological for the pragmatic necessities of a large diverse democratic republic. An intellectual and electoral hostage to the South, he defended that section's interests with every bit of executive power he commanded, and that was much more than has previously been recognized. His presidency did not suffer from feebleness or insufficient power or administration by a senile sixty-eight-year-old, as so many historians have argued. Buchanan was no mere executor of the laws; he was an activist chief executive. But the problem was that he used the power with such partiality for the South.

Years before, Buchanan had chosen sides in the great crisis of America's nineteenth century. Negligent about slavery but greatly attached to the values of southerners—especially their literal reading of the Constitution—he had surrounded himself with southerners in the cabinet, in the informal meetings of his administration, and even in his social life in Washington. As a result, he went beyond these associations not just to defend the South but to undertake a bitter crusade against the growing number of northerners who opposed slavery. He went beyond normal political custom by castigating Republicans as disloyal. And in Buchanan's mind because many northerners were anti-slavery, he held the North responsible for the disruptive sectional tensions. After all it was northerners who sent antislavery petitions to Congress and failed to return escaped slaves to the South. And it was northerners, with their free-soil, free-labor intentions, who had brought catastrophe (in his view) in Kansas. Clearly Buchanan's vision and inspiration for the future of the United States were increasingly at odds with most Americans, whose definitions of freedom and liberty did not include a slave republic dominated by a minority of slave owners.

Thus, when the crisis that was partly of Buchanan's making

occurred and South Carolina seceded, he did nothing. Suddenly this activist president offered the nation little more than the rhetorical exercise that secession was constitutionally illegal, but that he could do nothing about it. Of course this pronouncement served only to encourage the South. Yet there were a number of precedents for military action that the president could have followed, not just the better-known ones from Washington's and Jackson's administrations, but those from Taylor's and Fillmore's, when both presidents had threatened to call out the militia and use force against Texas in its border dispute with New Mexico.

To be sure, to do nothing was to do much, because Buchanan was granting the future Confederate States of America precious time to organize and prepare for war. By no means inevitable, the American Civil War remained contingent on various episodes, to which this intended peacemaker contributed as much as anyone. With Buchanan's mistakes, a confrontation that might have dwindled away into a minor action against one state became more certain. In this crisis three presidential failings—Buchanan's arrogance that he could achieve peace by being a partisan of the South, his ideological commitment to southern values, and his vision of the future with slavery gradually dying out—all came together to buttress a terrible presidential miscalculation.

So too did another fatal flaw—his dependence as a lonely bachelor on his mostly southern cabinet for social companionship. Even after South Carolina seceded, Buchanan continued to lend his ear to cabinet officers who were actively conspiring against the United States. He aided and abetted this process by meeting with officials who passed his plans on to secessionist leaders throughout the South. And in the crisis over Fort

Sumter, Buchanan listened to those voices as he formulated his own plans about how to keep the peace. He ordered Major Anderson to leave Fort Sumter and return to the indefensible Fort Moultrie, where the federal troops would promptly have been overrun by the South Carolina militia. Only the intervention of several cabinet officers changed the president's mind, although by this time Buchanan was too distraught to write the necessary memorandum. But when Buchanan had time to reflect on the matter after the war, he criticized Anderson for a move that most Americans thought saved the soul of the nation. Without Sumter the Confederates could have gone in peace. At first a self-confident chief executive, during the Sumter crisis Buchanan remembered the childhood warnings of his father and his own pessimism that every success was accompanied by a defeat. Drenched with confusion, for a time he became practically immobile.

In 1890, before he was elected president and had his own problems with presidential leadership, Woodrow Wilson set forth the ingredients of successful leadership in an essay titled "Leaders of Men." In a democracy, argued Wilson, persuasion was essential and had to be accomplished "by creeping into the confidence of those you would lead." Leadership required fairness as well. "Leadership for the statesman," he wrote, "is *interpretation*. [A leader] must read the common thought: he must test and calculate very circumspectly *the preparation* of the nation for the next move in the progress of politics."[1] All of Buchanan's presidential failings—his arrogant use of his power, his insistence on a vision that most Americans repudiated, his inflexible ideological support for the South, and his personal rigidity—can be summarized in Wilson's description. Ultimately Buchanan failed to *interpret* the United States.

Notes

1: ASCENSION—FROM STONY BATTER TO THE CABINET,
1791–1848

1. John Bassett Moore, ed., *The Works of James Buchanan* (New York: Antiquarian Press, 1960), 12:260 (All Buchanan quotes in the text are from this source.) George Ticknor Curtis, *Life of James Buchanan* (New York: Harper's, 1883), 1:3.
2. Curtis, 1:7.
3. Ibid., 18, 19.
4. Philip Klein, *President James Buchanan: A Biography* (University Park: Pennsylvania State University Press, 1962), 156; Curtis, 1:519.
5. Jonathan Ned Katz, *Love Stories: Sex Between Men Before Homosexuality* (Chicago: University of Chicago Press, 2001). I am indebted to King's biographer, Daniel Fate Brooks, for my understanding of the King-Buchanan relationship.
6. Elbert B. Smith, *The Presidency of James Buchanan* (Lawrence: University Press of Kansas, 1975), 13; *Congressional Directory of 1836*, 24th Cong.; James Sterling

Young, *The Washington Community* (New York: Columbia University Press, 1966).

7. Robert Remini, *Henry Clay: Statesman for the Union* (New York: W. W. Norton, 1991), 477; *Congressional Globe*, 27th Cong., 1st sess., 596.

8. Elizabeth Buchanan to James Buchanan, October 21, 1831 (Buchanan Papers, Historical Society of Pennsylvania).

9. *Polk: The Diary of a President, 1845–1849*, ed. Allan Nevins (New York: Longman's Green, 1929), 54, 27.

10. Ibid., 278, 306, 379.

11. Klein, 194.

2:    WHEATLAND TO THE WHITE HOUSE, 1849–1856

1. Klein, 208; Moore, 8:387; Curtis, 1:16.

2. Moore, 2:451.

3. Klein, 226.

4. Frederick Binder, *James Buchanan and the American Empire* (Selinsgrove, Pa.: Susquehanna University Press, 1994), 175, 17; Curtis, 2:100, 111; Moore, 9:158.

5. Moore, 9:95–96.

6. Curtis, 2:162, 120.

3:    THE BUCHANAN PRESIDENCY—THEORY AND PRACTICE

1. Moore, 8:496.

2. Don E. Fehrenbacher, *Slavery, Law, and Politics: The Dred Scott Case in Perspective* (New York: Oxford University Press, 1981), 168; Moore, 10:106–9; 13:39.

3. *The Diary of Edmund Ruffin* (Baton Rouge: Louisiana State University Press, 1981), 1:267.

4. Moore, 10:203.

5. Thomas Thomas to Alexander Stephens, in *Correspondence of Robert Toombs, Alexander Stephens, and Howell Cobb* (New York: Da Capo Press, 1970), 1:372.

6. Moore, 10:120; Kenneth M. Stampp, *America in 1857: A Nation on the Brink* (New York: Oxford University Press, 1990), 180.

7. Roy F. Nichols, *The Disruption of American Democracy* (New York: Macmillan, 1948), 130.

8. Moore, 10:190.

4: APPEASING THE SOUTH: THE FINAL MONTHS OF THE BUCHANAN PRESIDENCY

1. Mark W. Summers, *The Plundering Generation: Corruption and the Crisis of the Union, 1849–1861* (New York: Oxford University Press, 1987), 239–60; "The Covode Investigation," 36th Cong., 1st sess., House of Representatives, Report no. 648.

2. Curtis, 2:289; Moore, 10:461.

3. Nichols, 386.

4. William Brigance, *Jeremiah Sullivan Black* (Philadelphia: n.p., 1926), 301; Klein, 381; Philip Gerald Auchampaugh, *James Buchanan and His Cabinet on the Eve of Secession* (Lancaster, Pa.: privately printed, 1926); *Philadelphia Press,* September 10, 1883.

5. *Congressional Globe,* 36th Cong, 2nd sess., 1373.

AFTERWORD

1. *The Papers of Woodrow Wilson,* ed. Arthur Link (Princeton: Princeton University Press, 1969), 6:659.

Milestones

1791 Born in Stony Batter, Cove Gap, Franklin County, Pennsylvania, on April 23

1794 Family moves to Mercersburg, Pennsylvania

1809 Graduates from Dickinson College in Carlisle, Pennsylvania

1809–12 Studies law under James Hopkins in Lancaster, Pennsylvania

1814–16 Elected and reelected to Pennsylvania legislature as a Federalist

1819 Engaged to Ann Coleman, who breaks off the engagement

1820 Missouri Compromise passes Congress

1821–31 Member of House of Representatives; elected five times; becomes a Democrat

1828 Andrew Jackson elected president

1831 Appointed minister to Russia by Jackson

1833 Defeated for U.S. Senate seat

1834–45 Member of U.S. Senate, filling vacancy for the other Pennsylvania seat; reelected twice

1837 Chairman of Senate Foreign Relations Committee

1844 James K. Polk elected president

1845–49 Serves as secretary of state

1846 Senate ratifies Oregon Treaty; Mexican-American War begins

1849 Wheatland becomes his permanent residence; niece Harriet Lane moves there

1852 Loses Democratic nomination to Franklin Pierce, who is elected president

1853–56 U.S. minister to Great Britain

1854 Ostend Manifesto signed

1856 Elected president

1857 Dred Scott decision

1858 Lecompton constitution rejected on a third vote in Kansas; Minnesota admitted into the Union

1860 Abraham Lincoln elected president; South Carolina secedes; controversy over Fort Sumter begins

1861 Six more states secede during Buchanan's term; Lincoln inaugurated in March

1866 Publishes *Mr. Buchanan's Administration on the Eve of the Rebellion*

1868 Dies on June 1 and is buried in Lancaster

Selected Bibliography

Auchampaugh, Philip Gerald. *James Buchanan and His Cabinet on the Eve of Secession*. Lancaster, Pa.: privately printed, 1926.

Binder, Frederick Moore. *James Buchanan and the American Empire*. Selinsgrove, Pa.: Susquehanna University Press, 1994.

Birkner, Michael, ed. *James Buchanan and the Political Crisis of the 1850s*. Selinsgrove, Pa.: Susquehanna University Press, 1996.

Buchanan, James. *Mr. Buchanan's Administration on the Eve of the Rebellion*. New York: D. Appleton, 1866.

Coleman, John F. *The Disruption of the Pennsylvania Democracy, 1848–1860*. Harrisburg: Pennsylvania Historical and Museum Commission, 1975.

Crawford, Samuel. *The Genesis of the Civil War*. New York: Charles Webster, 1887.

Curtis, George Ticknor. *Life of James Buchanan: Fifteenth President of the United States*. 2 vols. New York: Harper's, 1883.

Fehrenbacher, Don E. *The Dred Scott Case: Its Significance in American Law and Politics*. New York: Oxford University Press, 1978.

Gara, Larry. *The Presidency of Franklin Pierce.* Lawrence: University Press of Kansas, 1992.

Gienapp, William E. *The Origins of the Republican Party, 1852–1856.* New York: Oxford University Press, 1988.

Holt, Michael F. *The Political Crisis of the 1850s.* New York: Wiley, 1978.

Johannsen, Robert W. *Stephen A. Douglas.* New York: Oxford University Press, 1973.

Klein, Maury. *Days of Defiance: Sumter, Secession, and the Coming of the Civil War.* New York: Vintage, 1999.

Klein, Philip S. *President James Buchanan: A Biography.* University Park: Pennsylvania State University Press, 1962.

Maizlish, Stephen E., and John J. Kushma. *Essays on American Antebellum Politics, 1840–1860.* College Station, Tex.: Texas A&M University Press, 1982.

Meerse, David E. "Buchanan, Corruption, and the Election of 1860." *Civil War History* 12 (June 1966): 116–31.

Moore, John Bassett. "Buchanan's Patronage Policy: An Attempt to Achieve Political Strength." *Pennsylvania History* 40 (January 1973): 37–57.

———. ed. *The Works of James Buchanan.* Vols. 1–12. New York: Antiquarian Press, 1960.

Murray, Robert K., and Tim H. Blessing. *Greatness in the White House: Rating the Presidents, Washington Through Carter.* University Park: Pennsylvania State University Press, 1988.

Nevins, Allan. *The Emergence of Lincoln.* 2 vols. New York: Charles Scribner's Sons, 1950.

———. *Ordeal of the Union: A House Dividing, 1852–1857.* New York: Charles Scribner's Sons, 1947.

———. *The Statesmanship of the Civil War.* New York: Collier Books, 1962.

Nichols, Roy F., and Philip S. Klein. "The Election of 1856." In *History of American Presidential Elections, 1789–1968,* ed. Arthur M. Schlesinger, Jr., and Fred L. Israel. Vol. 2. New York: Chelsea House, 1971.

Potter, David M. *The Impending Crisis, 1848–1861.* New York: Harper and Row, 1976.

———. *Lincoln and His Party in the Secession Crisis.* New Haven: Yale University Press, 1942.

Rauch, Basil. *American Interest in Cuba, 1848–1855.* New York: Columbia University Press, 1948.

Rawley, James A. *Race and Politics: "Bleeding Kansas" and the Coming of the Civil War.* Philadelphia: Lippincott, 1969.

Shenton, James P. *Robert John Walker: A Politician from Jackson to Lincoln.* New York: Columbia University Press, 1961.

Smith, Elbert B. *The Presidency of James Buchanan.* Lawrence: University Press of Kansas, 1975.

Stampp, Kenneth M. *America in 1857: A Nation on the Brink.* New York: Oxford University Press, 1990.

———. *And the War Came: The North and the Secession Crisis, 1860–1861.* Baton Rouge: Louisiana State University Press, 1950.

Summers, Mark W. *The Plundering Generation: Corruption and the Crisis of the Union, 1849–1861.* New York: Oxford University Press, 1987.

Index

U.S. Congress
  Buchanan as president and, 87,
    89, 105–6, 108, 124–25
  Buchanan in, 22, 24–25
  forts crisis and, 135, 139
  Kansas and, 93, 97, 100, 102–6,
    148–49
  Ostend Manifesto and, 66
  power of, 4, 147
  Republicans and, 106, 112–13,
    121
  slavery and, 32, 53–54
  war making powers of, 111
U.S. Constitution, 2, 4, 14, 24, 29,
    34, 50, 75–76, 138, 147, 150
U.S. House of Representatives, 1,
    23, 27, 103–4, 109, 112, 149
  Committee of Agriculture, 28
  corruption investigation and,
    113–16
  Judiciary Committee, 28–29
U.S. Senate, 1, 42, 21, 28–29,
    32–34, 112
  Committee on Territories, 101
  Committee on the District of
    Columbia, 34
  Foreign Relations Committee,
    34
  Judiciary Committee, 34
U.S. Supreme Court, 29
  Buchanan offered seat on, 1,
    38–39
  slavery and, 83–86, 119
Unionism
  Buchanan's contradictions and,
    71–72, 86, 117, 121
  Buchanan's, during war, 142–43
  Buchanan's turn toward,
    136–38
  in South, 141

Updike, John, 147
Utah crisis, 90–93, 106, 107

Van Buren, Martin, 30, 32, 34, 45,
    52
veto, 77, 117–18
Victoria, queen of England, 60, 61
Virginia, 51, 120, 139

"Wakarusa War," 96
Walker, Robert, 96–100
Walker, William, 110
War Department, 115, 135
War of 1812, 17, 18, 34, 98, 111
Washington, George, 11, 50, 76,
    126, 151
Washington, D.C., reinforcement
    of, 139–40
Washington Association, 17
Washington Constitution, 133
Washington Peace Conference,
    139
Washington Union, 104
Watergate, 130
Wayne, James, 85
Webster, Daniel, 28, 33, 35
Webster-Ashburton Treaty (1841),
    35
West Indies, 62
Wheatland, 47–51, 142
Whig party, 23, 45, 66, 76, 77
Whiskey Rebellion, 11, 126
Wigfall, Louis, 139
Wilmot, David, 55
Wilmot Proviso, 53, 55
Wilson, Woodrow, 13, 130, 152
Wyandotte constitution, 105

Yale Bread and Butter Riot, 13
Young, Brigham, 90–92

ABOUT THE AUTHOR

JEAN H. BAKER is professor of history at Goucher College. She is the author of several books, including *The Stevensons* and a biography of Mary Todd Lincoln, and she is at work on a book about the suffrage movement. She lives in Baltimore, Maryland.